HOW A RUSSIAN SPY LED AN AMERICAN JOURNALIST TO A U.S. DOUBLE AGENT

Simon & Schuster   New York   London   Toronto   Sydney   Singapore

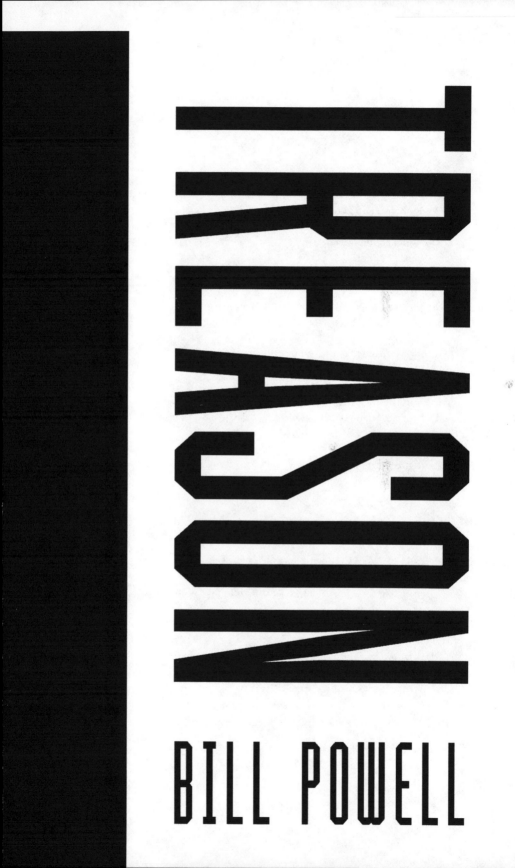

TREASON

BILL POWELL

SIMON & SCHUSTER
Rockefeller Center
1230 Avenue of the Americas
New York, NY 10020

For information regarding special discounts for bulk purchases,
please contact Simon & Schuster Special Sales at 1-800-456-6798
or business@simonandschuster.com

DESIGNED BY LISA CHOVNICK

Manufactured in the United States of America

10 9   8   7   6   5   4   3   2   1

Library of Congress Cataloging-in-Publication Data
Powell, Bill.
    Treason : how a Russian spy led an American journalist to a U.S. double
    agent/Bill Powell.
        p.   cm.
    Includes index.
    1. Baranov, Vyacheslav Maximovich. 2. Hanssen, Robert. 3. Powell, Bill.
4. Russia (Federation). Glavnoe razvedyvatel§'oe upravlenie—Biography.
5. United States. Central Intelligence Agency. 6. Spies—Russia (Federation)—
Biography. 7. Spies—United States—Biography. 8. United States. Federal Bureau
of Investigation. I. Title: How a Russian spy led an American journalist to a U.S.
double agent. II. Title.
UB271.R92 B377 2002
327.1247073'092—dc21   [B]   2002066989
ISBN 0-7432-2915-0

For Taro Powell,
who when he grows up
I hope decides to be something
other than a spy

ACKNOWLEDGMENTS

I'd like to thank Alice Mayhew and her able deputy Roger Labrie at Simon & Schuster, two of the best in the business, for all the care and time they put into editing this story. They really punched it into shape, and I couldn't have done it without them.

CONTENTS

CONTENTS

INTRODUCTION

Life as a foreign correspondent—particularly one working in places like Russia, where this story originates, or in China, where I worked until March of 2002—can be a funny business. Sometimes you work on stories for months and months, and they don't pan out. When I was Moscow bureau chief for *Newsweek,* from the summer of 1996 to the summer of 2000, I spent over a year and a half—and lots of *Newsweek's* money— pursuing a story of baby theft in a city in western Ukraine. Not baby selling, the now common practice in less developed countries of peddling orphans for adoption in the West for lots of money. This was baby *theft:* Several mothers who gave birth in a particular clinic were told their children were stillborn, that they had died during birth. They had not. They had been stolen and sold to couples who couldn't possibly have known—in the United States, France, and Israel, among other wealthy nations.

We never printed that story, though I will go to my grave believing it was true, because I couldn't nail it. Evidence promised by prosecutors in Ukraine was never provided to us. One, over an elegant dinner at a Kiev restaurant, flatly asked for a substantial bribe. Some of the mothers who were alleged victims in these scams were not quite credible. Ultimately, we couldn't pull the trigger. On a story like that, every "I" has to be dotted and "T" crossed. I didn't quite get there. My editors knew that was the nature of the beast, and never held the time and money I spent chasing the story against me.

I mention this because that is the second best story I have ever worked on—even if I never wrote it. I struggled and agonized and worked it to distraction, and finally killed it myself. It was the kind of investigative journalism that I think much of the reading public believes is typical of what we do.

Not always. Not usually, actually. The best story I ever worked on was entirely different. It took, in some senses, almost no initiative at all. As the Moscow bureau chief for *Newsweek,* I got myself in the middle of a mole hunt, a search by the U.S. government for a well-placed spy in our government who was on Moscow's payroll. A big, high-profile mole hunt, as it turned out. Sometimes, in places like Russia and China and no doubt elsewhere, a story takes hardly any effort. It can be right outside your window, as easy to see as it is to get up in the morning. Sometimes, in fact, the story just knocks on your door and walks into your office. Quite literally. What follows is one of those stories.

TREASON

CHAPTER 1

FIRST CONTACT

I do not, truth be told, remember the exact day Vyacheslav Baranov walked into my office in Moscow. It was the early summer of 1998, and I had been *Newsweek*'s bureau chief there for nearly two years, arriving just after Boris Yeltsin was re-elected in June of 1996 for what would turn out to be a disastrous second term.

But that someone like Baranov could just walk into our office unannounced, the fact that *anyone* could walk into our office unannounced, spoke to just how much Russia had changed since the collapse of the Soviet Union in 1991. Our office was on Kutuzovsky Prospekt, just up the broad, eight-lane thoroughfare from the Russian White House, which at the time of the collapse of the Soviet Union was the parliament, the place were Yeltsin famously stood atop a tank to save the revolution, and just down from the huge arch that commemorates Russia's rout of Napoleon. This was the middle of one of the world's most historic cities, and that history surrounds you.

During the Cold War, the big, impersonal diplomatic compounds on Kutuzovsky—if you've ever seen Co-op City in the Bronx, that's basically what they look like—were open only to diplomats and foreigners. Only Soviet citizens with special permission, such as those working for foreign journalists, were allowed in. And all of them had to report back to their government what it was we were up to. Phones in both the apartments and the offices were bugged, and journalists were, as a matter of course, followed whenever they ventured outside the compound.

Five years after the collapse of the Soviet Union, most of this had changed completely. While both our office and home phones were still bugged, we never got the impression anyone was listening anymore. Far from being a police state, Russia in the Yeltsin years tended toward anarchy; the fearsome state security *apparat* of the Soviet era had effectively been privatized, the best people snapped up by the businessmen, the so-called oligarchs who had come to dominate the post-Soviet economic landscape.

The ease with which absolutely anyone could stroll into what had once been forbidden ground for Soviet citizens was a small window on the anarchic quality Moscow had taken on. The people who would occasionally pitch up in our office were usually poor souls, destitute, mainly, some of them alcoholics, some of them seemingly paranoid. One poor old man named Nikolai, who spoke with a pronounced stutter, hounded me constantly with his tales that the KGB was still persecuting him—for reasons that were never clear. Another woman, a fine English speaker who claimed to have once worked for a United Nations agency, came in often to beg for a job with *Newsweek*. She was invariably drunk.

I felt sorry for all these people, and spent more time listening to their tales of woe than I should have. But even before Baranov turned up, I had grown irritated with my office manager for letting them just stroll into my office. It was ridiculous. I wasn't in a position to help them, and *Newsweek* wasn't paying me to spend quality time with cranks, however desperate they may be.

In the weeks before Baranov's first visit, my colleague in the office, a young British reporter named Owen Matthews, whom I had hired as a full-time stringer, had been poking into rumors that Russia still maintained a large and largely secret chemical weapons development program. At some point during the course of the reporting for this piece, he mentioned to me that he had gotten a couple of strange calls from a guy who claimed to be a former officer of the GRU—the once powerful, and, in the West, feared, Soviet military intelligence agency. He had said he wanted to visit the bureau and meet the *Newsweek* correspondents. Owen at one point wondered aloud whether this wasn't some form of harassment from the current

Russian security agencies, who may not have been thrilled that he was trying to dig up information about the alleged chemical weapons program. I don't remember what I said, but I remember thinking I didn't believe that. The story hadn't progressed that far, and I had already concluded that the newly constituted KGB, known now as the FSB (Federal Security Bureau), wasn't spending a lot of time worrying about what foreign correspondents were up to.

So when the latest of the line of strangers to show up in my office came in late one afternoon, I just thought to myself, Here we go again. He looked to be in his sixties. Thin, gaunt almost, about five feet eight inches tall, bald save for swathes of white hair on each side of his head, the only thing that registered immediately about him was the quality of his English. He spoke with a slight Russian accent, but almost flawlessly. His gauntness, and the fact that his face was deeply lined and his teeth had deteriorated, suggested that he had endured some hard times. But that was only true for about the entire Russian male population.

He came in saying he was looking for Andy Nagorski, who had been my predecessor as the Moscow bureau chief. I politely told him that Andy and I had swapped jobs almost two years before, and that Andy was now the Berlin bureau chief. I was curious why he wanted to see Andy. He replied that he had been a prisoner at Perm 35, an infamous labor camp in the Urals where many Soviet dissidents had been imprisoned, and that a few years into his time there, Andy had visited with a group of former dissidents.

This was true. Nagorski had done a piece on what life was like in these infamous camps, and it centered around a visit to Perm 35. I still didn't quite understand why he wanted to see Andy, but I asked him why he was in there.

He was sparing on the details in that first visit. But he did say that he had been imprisoned for espionage. That he had been a colonel in the GRU, and that in 1989, while based in Dhaka, Bangladesh, he had agreed to spy for the CIA. Upon his return to Moscow sometime later, he had been arrested, tried, and convicted. And then had done time in Perm 35, where, he added, he had spent some of his time translating Frederick Forsyth spy novels from English into Russian.

I don't know whether it was clear to him in that first meeting, but I didn't believe any of this. I had, in my short time in Moscow, already become jaded. I believed he had been in Perm 35 when my colleague visited, but I didn't believe the espionage tale. First, I didn't know whether the Russians imprisoned spies at Perm 35. I had thought, in fact, that the Russians took their spies to the basement underneath KGB headquarters, at what was once Felix Dzherzhinsky Square (named after the founder of the Soviet secret police) and put a bullet in the back of their heads. Second, I cynically sensed, given my previous visitors, a sob story coming and a request, at some point, for money.

I didn't know how right, and how wrong, I was.

Because I didn't know where this story was headed—indeed, because I was so skeptical of his tale that he wasn't at that point a "story," he was a crank—these early days are a bit of a blur. Baranov himself says he doesn't remember how long after that initial visit it was before he called me again. But it wasn't long. Maybe a week; maybe ten days. The one thing that had stuck in my mind was the Nagorski detail. If this guy was telling tall tales, it wasn't all a tall tale. He clearly had been at Perm 35 for something, otherwise how would he know Andy had been there, unless he had read it in *Newsweek* (not very likely given the magazine's limited circulation in Russia). Plus, his English was extraordinarily good, and he was intelligent, distinguished even. I was at some level intrigued. And so when he called again, I said sure, come by.

We met again in my office. And this time, after some small talk, he began to add more details to his story. He said he had wanted to meet Andy or someone from *Newsweek* because he wanted to get in touch with the U.S. government. He had been trying to do so on his own since he had been released from prison several months earlier. He had gotten nowhere. He said he had, through a friend who had emigrated from Ukraine to Canada, got the name of the FBI legal attaché at the U.S. Embassy in Ottawa. A man named Jerry Rose. He had sent faxes to Jerry Rose several times, explaining his situation, explaining that he wanted, needed, to get in touch with the U.S. government. Jerry Rose had never responded.

Why didn't you just go to the U.S. Embassy here, in Moscow? I asked. He said he was concerned, first, that that might be risky. He had done his time, but the Russian government still had his passport. He couldn't travel out of the country; and if his government's spies discovered him walking into the U.S. Embassy, having already been convicted for espionage, he could get into trouble all over again.

This sounded reasonable. Russian spies may not have been paying attention to journalists anymore, but they no doubt still had people checking out who was going in and out of the U.S. Embassy.

I asked Baranov why he hadn't just been killed on the spot, once "convicted" of espionage. He said that had he been "tried" under the law of the Soviet Union, his sentence would have been harsher. But his trial had come after the Soviet Union had fallen. He came under the law of the newly con- stituted Russian Federation. And since the state had been un- able to prove that he had given away secrets "highly damaging" to the country's security, he had received a relatively lenient prison sentence.

These answers came calmly, straightforwardly. I think it was during this second meeting that the thought first occurred to me: if this guy is making this up, he's a helluva good liar. It was the first moment when I thought that maybe he wasn't making it up.

I asked why he thought the U.S. government, at that point in the person of Jerry Rose, hadn't responded to his requests for contact. He demurred, said he didn't know. Why, I asked, was it so important that he get in touch?

I wasn't taking notes at this second meeting, but it was then, for the first time, that he let me know that he felt he had been treated badly—both after he had been recruited in Bangladesh, and after he had been released from the Gulag. He had a grievance, and he wanted to air it.

That was not to be the only reason he wanted to talk to the U.S. government, as I would learn soon enough. But now his motivation in coming to the *Newsweek* office (if he was telling the truth) was becoming clear. He wanted me, someone with access to U.S. diplomats in Russia, to help him gain access to them. He hadn't said that yet, nor did I know then how deep his anger ran. I didn't know then the details of *how* he'd been handled—or mishandled. Nor did I know why, if he was telling the truth, he had agreed to spy for the Americans. But as he spoke, not very specifically, about what had happened to him, the thought first entered my head: not, could I help this guy? Not, *should* I help this guy? I wasn't even considering the idea at this point that I would end up where I eventually did, smack in the middle of a mole hunt. No, at that point I was simply intrigued. Not convinced, but intrigued. If Vyacheslav Baranov was to be believed, if he was telling me the truth, this might be a helluva story. That was the thought that popped into my head.

Was he telling the truth? I had made it clear to him, if only through my willingness to listen at this point, that I was interested in what he was saying. I wanted to hear more. I reinforced the point just before he left that day. If you want to continue to talk, I'd be happy to. Just call and let me know when you want to come by.

He thanked me, and said something to the effect that he'd probably do just that. If I needed to figure out whether he was telling the truth, he needed to figure out if I could, and would, actually help him.

CHAPTER 2

WHAT SPIES DO

Journalists and spies do not mix easily, even though we are, at some basic level, in the same business: gathering information, finding out things, and sending that information to a wider audience. In our case, to our readers; in their case, to governments. We also both try to get people to tell us things they probably shouldn't. For journalists that's sometimes hard, and all we have is our wits; we can try to cajole, or charm, or persuade someone that it really is in his or her interest to reveal something. Sometimes it works, sometimes it doesn't. When a source asks to be paid for information—as the Ukrainian prosecutor did when I was pursuing the baby-theft story—his credibility vanishes right before our eyes.

Spying is different. When spies try to recruit people to betray their countries, to provide information to an agent of a foreign country, they can cajole but they can also pay. And they can intimidate or blackmail if they happen to have compromising material on you. Journalists ideally want their sources to be identified, to speak "on the record" so as to enhance the credibility of a story. A spy's sources, of course, can never go public.

It is the secrecy of spying, and the relative transparency of journalism, that is at the heart of the tension between the two. That is why, in the relatively rare instances when U.S. intelligence agents are even willing to meet with foreign correspondents in places like Moscow or Beijing, there is not a lot the journalist can do with whatever information a spy provides. And in my experience, it was never much. There is no question that spies find things out that journalists don't (though you'd be surprised how often the reverse is true). The problem is, you don't know where a spy's information came from. He'll never tell you. Nor is it easy to assess why it is he's telling you anything. The agenda of an intelligence agent, or his sources, is rarely apparent. Some journalists are drawn to spies, trying to cultivate them as sources. I always thought they were drawn by the myth of spying, of the fictional derring-do, the seductive idea that they really must know interesting secrets and maybe, just maybe, they'll drop one on you.

No one from the CIA had ever told me anything interesting. But now I had a spy, a former spy anyway, in my midst; and he wasn't one of ours, but a former member of the fabled GRU, an agency that in its discipline, its secrecy, and (by reputation anyway) its effectiveness, surpassed the KGB.

As he had said he would, Baranov accepted my invitation for another meeting in the late summer of 1998, and by then our own dance had begun. He was the spy, and he would, over the next few months, try in his own way to "recruit" me: to get me to deliver him, in some fashion, to his former employer, the U.S. government. I, on the other hand, was cultivating him as a source; indeed, as the centerpiece of what could turn out to be a good story. That certainly wasn't on his agenda. And we were still a long way from the point where I would think of going to the U.S. government on his behalf. If I was ever going to go to the government at all, I thought, it would be when I was convinced Baranov was telling me the truth and had told me his whole story. Then I would go to the government and try to interview the appropriate people, those who had recruited him, who had handled him. Just to hear their side of it. In order to be able to write it all. Not until much later would I realize what I was getting sucked into. I was intrigued with this guy's tale. It might be a story. We'll see.

In our third meeting, and indeed in many of those that followed, Baranov was not all business. He seemed, in fact, a little lonely. He also obviously liked to use his English, and was widely informed about issues both within Russia and abroad. He would often talk about the articles he had read in *Newsweek*. If he was recruiting me, and he was, this was a soft sell.

But it had its effect. A man who betrays his country is probably not going to have many friends left. Particularly in the former Soviet Union in the mid-1990s, when lots of people, thanks mainly to their economic destitution, were pining for what they were beginning to think of as the good old days of the U.S.S.R. It was not as if Baranov's former pals in the

GRU were inviting him out to slug back vodka with them when he got out of Perm 35. A traitor living in his own country is a lonely man.

His awareness of and interest in what was going on around the world also, as spies say, fit the profile. I remember him in that third meeting speaking about living in Dhaka, Bangladesh, where he was posted by the GRU and where, as he would later tell me, he was first recruited by the CIA. I had been to Bangladesh once, and everything he said certainly squared with my impressions of the place. By this point, my skepticism about the broad contours of his story had pretty much evaporated. He certainly didn't appear to be making stuff up. I was becoming convinced that what he was telling me was probably true. That he had been a spy. That he had spent time in Perm 35. And that therefore he must have been caught doing something pretty egregious, like spying for the United States. I had dismissed the thought that he was a crank. He had, even without providing many details, established his bona fides, at least in my eyes.

Now I wanted the details. And I wanted to convince him that his story would be worth my telling. And that my interest served his agenda. He was smart enough to know that at some point my pursuit of this would lead me to the U.S. Embassy. And that, he fervently hoped, would be the beginning of what he wanted, an explanation, as he then put it, for what had happened. I did not realize at that point what he really meant by that. I had thought "an explanation" meant an apology, and indeed, that was part of it. And it also probably meant some money, and maybe relocation to the United States. Surely, if his story was true, he was owed that.

I figured that was it; that's all he was talking about. That's all there was to this. It showed how ignorant I was. Baranov wanted to hear the CIA's explanation for what happened to him not only for those reasons. Yes, he wanted money; but as much as anything, he wanted to hear the agency's explanation because he wanted to see if it squared with his own suspicions. Someone within the U.S. espionage community had betrayed him, he believed. His arrest was not the result of crack counterintelligence work by the KGB. He didn't know who it was who betrayed him, but he wanted to find out. It was possible, he conceded, that it was Aldrich Ames, the infamous former CIA officer who had been responsible for the deaths of at least twelve Soviets who were American spies in the former Soviet Union. But at that point he didn't know that for sure. Not by a long shot.

In its checkered history, the tale of Ames, finally arrested and convicted in 1994, while Baranov sat in a bleak transfer prison before going to Perm 35, was perhaps the blackest moment for the CIA until September 11, 2001, when it and the rest of the U.S. intelligence community failed to get wind of the most horrific attack ever launched on the United States of America, and nearly three thousand people died at New York's World Trade Center and at the Pentagon.

Ames had been a feckless, alcoholic, career CIA officer. Undistinguished professionally, he had managed to fail upward, mainly because he was one of the boys in what was at its core an insular, arrogant old–boys network. At the peak of his career, he was responsible for counterintelligence for the entire Soviet bloc—making sure that the agents the United States had recruited in the Soviet Union and Eastern Europe were real (as opposed to double agents feeding disinformation) as well as deterring Moscow's efforts to sign up U.S. intelligence officers at home. Ames, after agreeing to spy for the Soviets, enjoyed an immediate and stunningly obvious improvement in his standard of living. Most famously, he began commuting from a newly purchased, expensive home in Virginia to the CIA's headquarters in a Jaguar. No one, within what was supposed to be the best spying agency in the world, noticed. It took years for anyone at the agency to pay Ames's new affluence any mind. Finally, nine years and $2.7 million in his bank account after he first signed on with the Soviets, a joint FBI-CIA task force had arrested him. Aldrich Ames immediately became a symbol of the CIA's incompetence, and while, like most Americans, I was familiar with the broad outlines of his story, I had no idea, in the late summer of 1998, how important his story would become to the one I was tentatively beginning to pursue.

When I next met Baranov, I made it clear to him that this was now business for me. Mostly convinced that he was legit, I was no longer sure, despite the general chaos of the Kutuzovsky compound, that I wanted him sauntering into the office all the time. I didn't know where this was headed, but for the moment

I decided it wasn't wise to have a former GRU-colonel-turned-CIA-spy visiting the *Newsweek* office. The office was bugged, and if there was the slightest chance that anyone *was* listening, well, then it obviously wasn't a good idea to be talking there.

Instead, at the next meeting, we met across the street, at the John Bull Pub, one of several imitation British pubs that had sprung up in the New Moscow. Baranov agreed that this was probably a good idea. So one evening in the early autumn of 1998, I ducked under the pedestrian underpass that was just outside our office and went across the street to meet him at the bar. This time I brought a notebook with me, and when we sat down, I said simply that I wanted to start asking him all the questions that had begun to pile up in my head.

He had not agreed to be "interviewed," and we still hadn't had a serious discussion about my writing this. But when I started taking notes, he didn't blanch.

First things first, I said; I want to know who you are, where you grew up, who your parents were, and how you got into the GRU to begin with.

He nodded, took out one of his cigarettes (he had been a chain smoker for years), and calmly began to talk for the first time in detail about his life, about how he had come to where he was. I suspect he understood at that meeting that he may have found his lifeline.

CHAPTER 3

HOW YOU GET TO THE GRU

Vyacheslav Maximovich Baranov was born in Mogilev, a small city in Belorussia, the former Soviet republic due west of Russia. His life, like that of so many Soviet men of his generation, was forever marked by what the Russians call the Great Patriotic War—the fight against the Nazis that claimed one in five men in the U.S.S.R. from 1939 to 1944. His father, a railway official, was evacuated to the city of Saratov on the Volga so he could fight against the Germans when the war began in 1939. Five years later, as the Germans retreated from the eastern front, the Baranovs' first child, Tamara, was killed in a forest fire set by the Nazis as they fled. Baranov's mother was devastated by the loss of her daughter. For nearly three months she ate almost nothing and was severely ill when her husband returned from the war in 1944. He convinced her that they should have more children as a way to deal with their grief. She agreed, and in 1945 and again in 1947, she gave birth to boys—Valery, now a lawyer in Kamchatka, and then Vyacheslav. Neither would get to know their father. Not long after his return from the front he was diagnosed with leukemia, from which he died on January 2, 1949, in a Moscow hospital. Baranov's mother, still young and attractive, would never remarry, preferring, Baranov would recall many years later, "to live like many widows at the time in our country—in great need, often in misery, but preserving their dignity and faithfulness to the memory of their late husbands."

Baranov's fatherless childhood was thus fairly typical for boys of this era. The mother and the two boys were poor but not quite destitute. There was food on the table, and electricity and heat in the crowded, communal flat in which he and his brother grew up. (Communal flats, still common to this day in cities throughout the former Soviet Union, often house as many as five families in a single unit, with everyone sharing everything.) As ever, if you don't know of anything better, what you have doesn't seem so bad. Baranov spent his youth playing soccer and volleyball, but was also inclined, unlike his brother and many of their friends, toward academics. He did well in school and found that he had a knack for languages. He dabbled in German as a primary school student and then studied English intensively for six years, reading voraciously as he gained fluency.

In the postwar period in the Soviet Union, for poor young men whose families had no particular connections within the Communist Party hierarchy, there were few more attractive options than a career in the military. The victory over Hitler, and the extraordinary losses suffered by the Red Army, made the armed forces a deeply respected, almost sanctified institution. (There was some irony in this, of course. Part of the reason the Soviets lost so many men during the war, as historians during the glasnost period would later point out to their fellow citizens for the first time, was that many of its generals were incompetent, and that Stalin's battle plans most often consisted simply of throwing more and more young men at the Nazis.)

With the Cold War in full swing, the military's power, and its access to resources over which the state had total control, were unrivaled. The state mandated a period of military service for all young Soviet men, but Baranov wanted a career as an officer. And he was confident enough, even at that young age, that he would make it. "I remember bragging to my brother that I would be a fighter pilot," he said.

After finishing the Soviet equivalent of high school, he gained admission to the Suvorov Military School in Minsk. There, over the next seven years, he would develop a lifelong passion for aviation and in particular for jet fighters. He shared that interest with a classmate, Dmitry, a Ukrainian who would also end up in the Soviet air force, and one of the few friends who stuck by him through his humiliating arrest and jail sentence. That friendship would later prove critical as Baranov's effort to come in from the cold—to meet with his U.S. handlers again and find out what happened—neared an end.

After graduating from the Suvorov academy, Baranov enrolled in an elite air force flight school in the Ukraine. There, in 1969, he met Tatyana Sergeyevna, a beautiful student with whom he fell instantly in love. (Some thirty years later, on a visit to Perm 35 in the Urals where Baranov was imprisoned, one of the guards there would remark to me, unprompted, about what "a beautiful woman" his wife was: "Whenever she visited, everyone noticed." Tatyana was in her late forties at the time.)

They were a natural match. Baranov himself was handsome, athletic, and doing well in his course work. A man destined to become an officer in the Soviet military would be attractive to many Soviet women in the postwar period—particularly someone like Baranov, who didn't drink much and has an innately gentle bearing. Though he was headed for a career as a fighter jock, flying Soviet MIGs and preparing for war against the NATO enemy, Baranov didn't really fit the *Top Gun* stereotype. He was neither brash nor particularly macho. "Quiet, smart, and polite" was how a classmate described him. Within a year after he graduated from the institute, Baranov married Tatyana.

His dream of becoming a pilot had become real. At the air force flight-training school he took to the skies, and again was quickly noticed by his superiors for his intelligence, studiousness, and willingness to follow orders. Baranov remembers that time fondly. He considered himself a "patriot" who was fortunate: he was on track to be an officer, he thought, and engaging his passion for modern aircraft at the same time. He was also married to a woman he loved, and they would soon start a family. He wasn't living well, materially speaking (the couple lived in a cramped apartment, just two rooms and a small kitchen, on an air base), but by Soviet standards, life wasn't bad at all.

At this point, there is nothing about Baranov's life or career that would in any way foreshadow what was to come, that he would eventually end up betraying his country, on the eve of its collapse. Far from it, in fact. In June 1970, Baranov, having graduated from flight-training school, was assigned to an air base in the Soviet republic of Latvia. Now the father of his first daughter, Baranov routinely flew the MIGs he had dreamed about, and continued to impress his commanders with his quiet competence.

Though the Red Army had been the most favored arm of the services in the Soviet Union after the war, during the Cold War the Strategic Rocket Forces—which oversaw Moscow's growing arsenal of nuclear weapons—and the air force both rose in prominence. A series of Soviet leaders, beginning with Nikita Khrushchev, insisted that the Soviets keep up with the United States technologically, and in military terms, that meant in the air. From *Sputnik* to Yuri Gagarin's first-man-in-space flight and beyond, the Soviet air corps got enormous funding and increasing prestige. It would take a lot to lure someone like the young Vyacheslav Baranov out of the air force.

One day in 1975, Baranov was approached by an officer he had never met before, a Colonel Bakhar. The officer asked to talk, and the two sat down over tea in a study on the air base.

The colonel simply introduced himself as an air force officer, and then began to ask questions. It is said, Vyacheslav Maximovich, that you are proficient in languages and already speak English fairly well. True?

True.

How are you enjoying life in Latvia, and in the air force in general?

Baranov wondered what the point of the chitchat was, but it didn't last long. The "guest from Moscow," as Baranov's commanding officer had called Bakhar, quickly launched into a rigorous discussion of a wide range of subjects—military, political, geopolitical. Baranov had been initially unimpressed by his interrogator's "depressingly plain appearance," as he later put it, but by the time his two-hour session with Bakhar ended, that impression was gone. Bakhar was clearly a very smart man. And he, in turn, had been impressed with the young air force flyer. Before leaving, he suggested to Baranov that he take the examination required for entrance into the prestigious Military Diplomatic Academy in Moscow. If he did well enough, the colonel said, a career in military intelligence awaited.

It was called the Glavnoye Razvedyvatelnoye Upravlenie, and in the West came to be known simply as the GRU, the most secretive and, arguably, powerful intelligence agency in the Soviet Union. Lenin himself authorized the creation of the agency that was the GRU's forerunner in 1918, and that would in some way create the foundation for what would be the GRU's historic legacy: its secrecy, and its fierce independence from rival power blocs, including, most emphatically, the KGB, but also the Communist Party itself. Lenin set up the GRU to serve as a secret military intelligence service, separate and distinct from the Cheka, the ruthless secret police agency formed under the legendary Felix Dzherzhinsky that would be the forerunner of the KGB. In 1918 Lenin ordered Dzherzhinsky, to his fury, not to interfere in the work of the newly created GRU, and thus was the foundation for the historic rivalry between the two created. The Cheka famously infiltrated the GRU in 1919, and from then on it seems there was a deep-seated rivalry between the two agencies that makes the traditional rift in the United States between the CIA and the FBI look trivial.

Like the Red Army itself, the GRU emerged from World War II, the Great Patriotic War, with more prestige and thus more power and independence than ever before. The KGB was quietly hated by many Soviet citizens at home. It was, after all, the domestic iron fist of a brutally repressive regime, accountable to no one except a few men at the highest level of the politburo. But if, as Viktor Suvorov wrote in a groundbreaking 1984 book, *Inside Soviet Military Intelligence,* the KGB's task was "not to allow the collapse of the Soviet Union from the inside," the GRU's mission was to "prevent the collapse of the Soviet Union from the *outside.*" This distinction meant that the GRU, to the extent that it was known at all, was not an agency that generated fear and loathing within the country. It was widely seen, Suvorov and others have said, as a place for patriots rather than scoundrels. Indeed, contrary to the widespread perception, fed by decades of Cold War spy-versus-spy fiction and nonfiction, the KGB was not the most powerful arm of Soviet intelligence abroad. The GRU was—by far. Its interests encompassed not only military affairs but the politics and economics that underlay them in every country in which GRU agents were present. "There wasn't a whole lot," Baranov would recall years later, "that it wasn't interested in." And partly for that reason, and again contrary to the Karla myth conjured up by John Le Carré, GRU officers generally in the Cold War period tended to be better trained and educated than their KGB counterparts.

Baranov was aware of the GRU, of course, but had little knowledge of its workings and no idea it had been interested in him as a possible candidate for its ranks.

But it was. The agency higher-ups went after the elites, the best of the officer corps in training. They identified them early and got those they wanted. To refuse an offer to join the elite crew of GRU spies would be to put an effective end to any chance of rising through the ranks of the military. The GRU made offers that weren't often refused.

Baranov's visit from Colonel Bakhar, the visitor from Moscow, meant that he was one of the chosen, that he was under consideration for service in Soviet military intelligence, and this would put a quick end to his career as a fighter jock, and in the air force. It would require, as Bakhar told him, a stint at the military academy in Moscow—more English, a lot of tradecraft. He was told to "think about it," but there was nothing to think about. He knew it would do his military career no good to refuse. And in truth, he wasn't uninterested. The possibility of a life abroad was enticing. He had always read widely, even as a boy, and had more knowledge and curiosity about the world outside Soviet borders than most of his fellow citizens.

The GRU had come for a new recruit, and at the end of his meeting with the visitor from Moscow, in a dingy office on a remote air base in Latvia, Baranov and Bakhar shook hands. His future plans, Baranov knew then, had been radically altered.

CHAPTER 4

THE ROAD TO DHAKA

Unlike the storied KGB building, which sits conspicuously in the center of Moscow at what, during the Soviet era, was known as Dzherzhinsky Square, the headquarters of the GRU is located in what was once a central Moscow airport known as Khodinka field. It is enclosed on three sides, and in the late Soviet era housed several military research institutes, an aerodrome used for testing aeronautic equipment for the military, and, at the very center of the airfield, a nine-story rectangular building, made of the soulless gray concrete and glass that make so many cities and towns across the former Communist landscape look so much alike. The building had gone up in the late 1960s and was originally to house a military hospital. But after construction, the brass decided it was inadequate. Hearing that a brand-new building was available, the leadership of the GRU jumped at the chance to move from its relatively cramped

quarters on the Arbat in central Moscow. At first the Soviet citizens who lived in the neighborhood had no idea that their
new neighbor was one of the most powerful and secretive intelligence agencies in the world. Over time, however, everyone
came to know, because more and more GRU officers moved
into the surrounding apartment blocks. Security, however, was
airtight. According to Viktor Suvorov, not even the general secretary of the Communist Party or the minister of defense
could drive a car into this compound without it being stopped
for a thorough inspection.

At the height of its power in the late 1970s and early
1980s, the GRU consisted of sixteen departments (or "direc-
torates," as the Soviets called them) employing over five thousand senior bureaucrats and spies. And on a warm spring day in
1979, another young, bright recruit was admitted into their
midst. Vyacheslav Baranov was not without second thoughts
on that day, he would later admit. His cherished dream of
being an airman was over; so too was the relatively simple military life he and his family had gotten used to. He was curious
about the world, eager to see it, and not without some youth-
ful patriotic fervor. Tatyana had voiced her reservations about
the move, but she, like her husband, knew that to refuse was
not realistic.

So to Moscow it was for all the new recruits for a meeting
with the academy's then director, General Aleksei Pavlov, a legendary figure within Soviet espionage and one mostly of mystery to the West. Baranov says he does not remember much
from the speech given that day, the usual palaver, apparently,

about serving the motherland, and about how the Soviet Union's enemies were at once everywhere and tireless. The Soviet military was the motherland's first line of defense, the director said, and the GRU was her eyes and ears. And it was interested in everything that might affect the military balance in any country in which Moscow had an interest, which was to say, in those days, practically every country in the world.

But Baranov, like the other inductees, would not be sent out into that world for a while. The GRU viewed itself as a more serious espionage organization than the rival KGB, and thus the training for its new recruits was rigorous—far more so than that given to new recruits at the CIA's fabled "Farm" in Virginia, where freshmen joining the DO (Directorate of Operations), or covert operations arm of the agency, get all of about six months of work in tradecraft.

Baranov, already more than proficient in English, would spend a year honing his language skills while getting drilled, for another several months, in the black arts of espionage: surveillance; how to tell if you are being tailed; how to lose a tail; how to identify a location for a dead drop; how to execute a dead drop; how to pick one up; and communications, cryptography, and the codes used to communicate with field agents and with headquarters. The list, it seemed to Baranov, appeared endless. But this was graduate school at a very elite institution. The GRU prided itself on its tradecraft, on the discipline of its agents and the way they executed missions. His instructors would let on that they viewed KGB agents as second-rate practitioners, for the most part, of the essential skills an agent needed to possess; and of the enemy, well, not much was said, but this much was implicit—if you followed what was drilled into you at the GRU's version of the Farm in Moscow, you should never be blown as an operative.

The working assumption, Baranov recalls, "was that the enemy was not that good. We of course at the time did not know why that seemed to be the opinion. Sometimes among the other classmates we would talk about this and wonder whether it was just arrogance on our instructors' parts." Years later, sitting in a prison camp in the Urals, Baranov would recall those conversations bitterly, having eventually come to his own very firm conclusions as to just how skilled "the enemy" was.

In June Baranov, like all those who had made it through boot camp for spies, was given his GRU insignia, something that would, given the covert nature of his work, rarely if ever be worn.

The GRU told Baranov his cover would be as a foreign trade representative, what the U.S. diplomats call a commercial attaché. The Soviet military, of course, had an intense interest in the weaponry and technology available to the NATO countries and their allies (just as, of course, the United States and its allies had in Soviet weaponry). Being able to evaluate any part of NATO's weapons systems or military industrial infrastructure was a key part of the GRU's mission. It was also one of the most difficult. Getting access to meaningful data about the enemy's arsenal—blueprints, plans, or the technology itself— was not easy, even though the main target countries were the relatively open societies of the United States and its European allies.

Baranov was not in the field yet. With his background in aviation, and his passion for the technology of flying, he was assigned to a desk job in Moscow, assessing the intelligence that came in from the field about Western advances in aviation. It was an early lesson for him in how difficult it was to get useful information; the spy's trade, particularly in this realm, was not an easy one. "So much of what we'd get was from what were obviously public sources of information in the West: trade journals, engineering journals, that sort of thing," he said.

But even that made an impression, a glancing one, to be sure, at the time, but one that would eventually deepen, with enormous consequences for Baranov and his family. "The impression I had reading over that kind of material, the public information that would be sent to us from the West, was that these were very different societies from ours. There was information in those journals, not perhaps particularly sensitive information militarily, but much more than would ever be allowed to circulate freely in our country about fighter aircraft, and advanced radar systems, and that sort of thing. I was still young at the time, so I didn't know much, but I knew that this kind of information wasn't just floating around our country at the public library." At the time, Baranov says, his main reaction was that "this simply made our job a little easier. Not much, just a little. But I was also, I think, intrigued about how a country like the U.S., engaged in this ideological struggle, would allow this information to circulate. Intrigued, that's all."

Baranov found this work interesting for a while, but as some months passed, he began to weary of it. There was often very little to chew on, and he was beginning to get bored. Having been attracted mainly by the prospect of living abroad, he was eager to get his chance. And within a year or two, most new recruits are spun out to first assignments. Not necessarily to the romantic posts most agents in the GRU dreamed about—London, Paris, or Washington, the frontline capitals in the West. But for the GRU, and particularly in the pursuit of the West's military capabilities, the third world, as it was then known, was important territory. The Americans and the Soviets both had their client states, of course, and one of the benefits of having client states is that they would buy equipment from your defense contractors.

It would not be state-of-the-art equipment, of course, but in the third world the spying game could be very lucrative. Bureaucrats and military officials in poor countries could be bought. They leaked plans; they talked about discussions they had with weapons salesmen from the West, discussions about capabilities of new guidance systems, new planes, new artillery, you name it. And even if the information was about matériel a year or two behind what NATO was deploying itself, it was valuable to the Soviets (and vice versa, of course). "You could see what they had and project where they were going," as Baranov puts it.

So it would be in these battlegrounds—Africa, Southeast Asia, the Indian subcontinent—where new GRU agents tended to be placed for first assignments. And Baranov was more than game. Even Tatyana, his wife, could tell he was bored, and both were wondering whether he was really cut out for the GRU. The sooner an overseas assignment came, the better, they felt. "You couldn't lobby for it, of course," Baranov said. "The chain of command was too strict for that; this was a military organization, after all. But I let my superiors know I was ready and eager to do my patriotic duty abroad. That's why I had been chosen in the first place, so I thought it was time to get on with it."

The GRU agreed. Baranov's immediate superior called him into his office and said Baranov's time in Moscow was coming to an end. Soon he would be informed of his first overseas assignment, and within a month he would need to be ready to leave Moscow.

CHAPTER 5

DHAKA

There are not many who would choose Bangladesh as a first assignment, a last assignment, or for that matter an assignment anywhere in between. A nation of ethnic Bengalis, split off from Pakistan with the help of Indian troops in a civil war in 1971, it has over the years become a symbol of third-world destitution. It seems at times an accursed place. Located between the Ganges and Brahmaputra Rivers, the country is subject every year to monsoons that lead to disastrous flooding in which thousands die. Ask people of a certain generation in the United States if they have heard of Bangladesh, and some will say, yes, they remember the war being on the news in the early 1970s. But most, if they say anything at all, will say they remember the Beatles, and the Concert for Bangladesh. And why was there a concert for Bangladesh? Because the country was, and remains, hideously impoverished.

Vyacheslav Baranov did not choose Dhaka as a first assignment. Relatively junior officers in the GRU were told where
to go, and what to do when there. But the truth was, during
the Cold War, Dhaka actually was not a bad place to be. The
Indian subcontinent was an important theater of the Cold War
and from the Soviet Union's standpoint, given its abject
poverty, a particularly strategic location. According to the Soviet catechism, millions of poor people by definition were ripe
for revolution, to throw off the shackles of oppressive capital-
ism and join the global socialist brotherhood.

Bangladesh, like India, was officially neutral during the
Cold War, but in fact tilted toward Moscow. The Soviet Embassy, and the housing compounds that surrounded it, were,
like many other embassies (though not America's), in a pleasant, leafy section of town. Here you would not find the "stump
boys" who congregated around the choked intersections of
this city of nearly ten million. Stump boys were young men
who had lost limbs in industrial or other accidents. If you were
stuck in Dhaka at an intersection in a cab or, God forbid, a *tuk-
tuk,* the open-air, three-wheeled little taxis that are everywhere
in south Asia, the stump boys would approach on crutches and
thrust their severed limbs into your window, or into your face,
desperate for a handout. To guilt-ridden, shocked Westerners,
or even citizens of the Soviet Union, this was, as you might
imagine, an effective tactic.

Neither Baranov nor Tatyana had ever lived anywhere outside the Soviet Union. She had barely heard of Bangladesh
when he told her that was where they were headed, and didn't

know what to think. At the meeting at headquarters, however, when Baranov was told that Dhaka was where he was headed, he was smart enough to know that it was not entirely bad news. Though he was older than most agents getting first field postings, he knew that the subcontinent, while not the front-line of the Cold War, was nonetheless prime territory, particularly for what his assignment was: first, as his "cover" as a commercial attaché, to help sell Soviet weaponry to a client state that was poor but willing; second, as a spy, to find out what both the NATO countries and the Chinese were up to, see if their weapons salesmen were coming (as they would), and find out what they were offering by recruiting (bribing) local officials—something that was quite easy in a country as poor and legendarily corrupt as Bangladesh then was.

The Baranov family settled in, moving into a comfortable apartment—much larger than their flat in Moscow—in the compound of the Soviet trade mission. His wife, to Baranov's relief, got over her initial shock at the poverty and squalor of the city, and began to appreciate what they had. For one thing, the price was right. The apartment was free, and everything else was relatively inexpensive. And, since Soviet diplomats were more the toast of the town than the Americans, there was the diplomatic social whirl, of which the Baranovs, a handsome couple, became very much a part. In time, they were able to save some money, and Baranov bought a used car, which he enjoyed puttering around town in. He and Tatyana used to drive to the market streets and search for bargains. All in all, Dhaka wasn't bliss, but it was better than expected.

For Baranov, part of the reason is that he once again was impressing his masters. His GRU station chief in the Dhaka station was a man named Vladimir Alekseyev. A man about ten years Baranov's senior, Colonel Alekseyev ran a GRU station that consisted of field agents, a cipher clerk, several translators, and secretaries. It was, like all GRU stations, a fiefdom unto itself, taking orders from no one—not the ambassador, nor (heaven forbid) the KGB *rezident,* or station chief.

On the surface, Baranov says he and his boss could hardly have been more different. Alekseyev was, like an awful lot of Soviet military men, the gruff macho type, the sort of officer who measured a man by how much vodka he could drink. (And Alekseyev could drink a lot.) Baranov always tried to keep his vodka swilling to a minimum, though in truth, by Russian standards, that could still on occasion mean enough to put most mortals under the table. Still, Baranov was quiet, almost cerebral, in contrast to his boss.

But beneath his macho military exterior, Alekseyev was a thoughtful, by-the-book intelligence officer. He saw that his newest charge was intelligent, knew he already spoke better English than most of his agents, and was impressed by Baranov's quiet diligence, just as, several years before, his superiors in the air force had been.

Alekseyev quickly gave Baranov a fair bit of slack. Though initially he concentrated mainly on his cover job, trying to establish his bona fides as a commercial attaché attached to the Soviet state-owned military sales organization, Alekseyev let him begin to try to recruit his own agents sooner than most

new arrivals. He was to concentrate on domestic targets—
Bangladeshis rather than third-world-country diplomats like
the military attachés at NATO embassies.

Baranov was not a natural at what the spies call the retail
level—at sidling up to prospective targets, gaining their confi-
dence, seducing them, and then closing the deal. He was quiet
and a little bit shy, but the fact is, in Dhaka it didn't matter that
much. While the CIA usually evaluated its field agents by how
many attempts they made at recruiting people (rather than the
quality of the information that its agents eventually produced),
the GRU (like the KGB) was smarter. It wasn't quantity that
counted, but quality.

That meant for Baranov, the pace wasn't that onerous. He
took his time, providing as much military and economic information as he could to the *rezident* and back to Moscow. The
GRU's appetite for any and all information was voracious.
Baranov had identified a high-ranking civilian whom he knew
dealt directly with foreign arms merchants. The man later went
on to achieve greater power within the government. He had
met him at one of a spy's prime hunting grounds—the man's
office.

That's one of the funny things about all the cloak-and-
dagger mythology about spying. A lot of it, and in particular,
the initial passes, are usually done pretty much out in the open,
in someone's office or at receptions where an awful lot of people know what the score is: who is really a diplomat, who is really an arms merchant, and who is really a spy. As Baranov and
other spies will tell you, you don't close deals there, but you

begin them. And so it was at a routine visit to his office that Baranov began recruiting the man he called Ahmed.

"It was surprisingly easy," he recalls. He introduced himself as a commercial attaché from the Soviet trade mission and said he understood that the two shared an interest in military technology. Yes, his target replied. Though it was his job to evaluate and purchase weapons systems for the Bangladesh military, he was educated as an aeronautical engineer. In fact, he said, "I consider myself an engineer first and a military officer second."

Baranov, as he recalls the episode, took the opening, saying he felt the same way. He spoke of his passion for flying, his interest in the technical aspects of aeronautics. All of this was genuine, and he could see that Ahmed was listening intently. On Ahmed's wall in his office was an organization chart of his ministry, complete with phone numbers of all the bureaucrats working there. Before this meeting, Baranov and Alekseyev had decided to use the chart as a sort of test, to see how willing Ahmed might be to exchange information for money. Baranov looked at the chart and told Ahmed he would be very interested in having a copy. Just having the direct phone numbers of the key people in the ministry would be of use to him as a trade attaché. And, of course, he added, I'd be willing to pay for it.

Baranov watched carefully how Ahmed reacted to this, and was pleased to see that he barely reacted at all. That would be no problem, Ahmed said, I can give you a copy right now. Baranov said he was very grateful and took out 500 takas, the local currency, then worth slightly more than $50. Baranov again watched Ahmed's reaction to this transaction carefully, and he could tell that his prospective agent was "disappointed." But that was good. The problem was the amount of money, not the transaction itself, and the GRU was willing to pay quite well, particularly by Bangladesh standards, for the information Ahmed had.

Within weeks, Baranov was able to take Ahmed out to dinner at a Chinese restaurant on the outskirts of town and near, of all places, the American Embassy, and make his pitch. He was very interested in the latest weaponry the Chinese government may have on offer. The competition was always active. Might there be a way to get a look at what the Chinese were peddling, which systems, and more importantly, their technical specifications?

Baranov says Ahmed didn't pause for long. There might be, he said. Then and there they struck an agreement. For cash payments, Ahmed would turn over whatever information he got from the competing arms merchants.

"It wasn't electrifying stuff," Baranov says, "but it was what we were supposed to do in our respective areas. Find out what the other guys were doing. What they were selling." There were no huge technological secrets turned over, but Baranov's boss was very pleased, and so too were the officers back at headquarters. Though perhaps not a natural-born spy, Baranov had shown he could do the job: pitch a potential informant, and then close the deal. "It's what spies do," he would say years later, and he had accomplished his task within a year and a half of his arrival in Dhaka. This was no mean feat. At the academy, the man who taught Baranov "strategic intelligence," a famous spy named Vladimir Zotin, had told the class that only about 10 percent of the time do field operatives succeed in the primary mission of recruiting a valuable asset. As Baranov would later say, "persuading a man to betray his country is usually not an easy thing to do."

If you were a spy for the Soviet Union, or for the United States of America, there was one other thing you did: you watched the other guys always and intently. You found out who their agents were in a given station, and kept an eye on them. You watched whom they tried to pitch, and they did the same. It didn't matter where. London, Washington, Moscow, Khartoum, Dhaka. There were few places in the world that weren't, during the Cold War, part of the battlefield, at least as far as spying was concerned. Baranov, in the mid-1980s in Dhaka, was happy enough. But that, over time, would change. And he soon would come face-to-face with the enemy, and learn what the spying game is really about.

CHAPTER 6

VOLLEYBALL IN THE SHADE

For centuries, diplomacy, and all the rules and niceties that are supposed to go along with it, have provided the veneer of civility for the ugly realities of spying, for the efforts spies make to steal secrets and to get men to betray their countries. During the Cold War, in third-world fronts like the south Asian subcontinent, no less than in Washington or Moscow, spies socialized with each other fairly frequently. While our governments plotted nuclear strategy and fought proxy wars in Southeast Asia, Afghanistan, and Central America, our spies played volleyball with each other.

At least they did in Dhaka, Bangladesh. The Soviet Embassy was hosting a friendly tournament for its fellow diplomats in the summer of 1988, and the United States was invited. This, given the heat of the Dhaka summer, was decidedly not spike-it-down-their-throats volleyball; it was backyard stuff, volleyball with lots of beer breaks.

Most of the players were regular diplomats. But not all. One of the Americans in attendance was a young man named Brad. He was a quiet, diligent agent who at the time was well liked at the Directorate of Operations back in Langley. They viewed him as a comer, and in an era when the agency was not having great success recruiting valuable agents, he had consistently shown a calm, persistent bedside manner.

During the course of the game—which Baranov recalls the Soviet side won easily ("the Americans were not very good players, I'm afraid to say, though we were impressed by how hard they tried")—Brad struck up a conversation with the GRU officer. Just chitchat at the start, each sticking with their "covers"—Brad was a diplomat and Baranov a foreign trade official—but each knowing the truth. Later, as the afternoon was drawing to a close, Brad drew Baranov aside, and this time signaled that he meant business. He asked Baranov whether he and another colleague from the Soviet mission might be able to come to his house for dinner. Baranov was taken aback because the other man Brad invited was also a member of the GRU station. This, he remembers thinking, could hardly be a coincidence. He parried, pleading that he was "hellishly busy" so maybe another time.

Brad backed off, handed Baranov a phone number, and said he hoped they could stay in touch. He added that he didn't think a dinner meeting should be out of the question. Baranov didn't respond, but took the number and put it in his pocket.

This is the first time an American spy had made a pass at Baranov. He was surprised by it but not uninterested. He worried, though, because at one point he thought he noticed a resident KGB officer watching him while he was talking to Brad. He wondered if that alone might draw suspicion. To cover himself, he reported the pass to the *rezident*—standard procedure for any intelligence agent that the opposition takes a run at.

But for anyone in the Soviet secret services, the mid- to late-eighties was a time of increasing turmoil, something that the CIA and other Western intelligence agencies barely had a whiff of. At the time both the KGB and the GRU, like the rest of the country, suffered from what was an increasingly serious economic crisis. Budgets were tight and getting tighter. Jobs in the field were not getting filled, leaving more work for the agents who were out there, including the paperwork that they all dreaded but which the GRU, like most spy agencies, insisted on: written reports on virtually any encounter they had with locals, and with other diplomats, of course. And also reports that lent credence to their cover jobs—in Baranov's case, economic analyses and selling military aircraft to Bangladesh.

But far from having computers on which to file their reports back to Khodinka, the GRU field agents typed them on old Soviet-made typewriters. When at one point the ribbon on his ran out, the embassy didn't have any spare ones in stock. Baranov went out and bought a new typewriter himself, using his own money.

Money was becoming a constant problem for Baranov's agency, one that had by the mid-eighties begun to sap morale among the GRU officers in the field. Pay raises that had been promised didn't come through. The living quarters in the Soviet compound had gotten seriously run-down. Baranov says he would gently remind Tanya, his wife, that things were hardly going to be better at home, and indeed, that was an understatement. Everything from the quality of the food to the size of their apartment was still far superior in a diplomatic compound in Dhaka, Bangladesh, than it would have been for them back in Moscow or virtually anywhere else in the Soviet Union.

Still, nearly two years into his stint in Dhaka, these day-to-day problems began to bug Baranov. In his own mind, he listened to the propaganda coming from Moscow about the Soviet system's economic superiority, and how the West was always on the verge of some great economic crisis, and he found it increasingly embarrassing. In this he would be like millions of his countrymen at the time, people for whom the outlandish claims their government made had gone from being the stuff of daily cynical jokes, to the source of a simmering anger.

Very much for these reasons, of course, Mikhail Gorbachev had come to power promoting both glasnost, a new openness that allowed a measure of freedom of complaint, as well as perestroika, an economic restructuring. He thrilled the West and at the beginning stirred optimism among young officers in the GRU. "Most intelligence officers are not stupid," Baranov would say later. "We could see with our own eyes what the true situation was in our country. And beside the few hardcore

Stalinists who were left in our service, everyone wanted a little freedom. It's only natural."

But the excitement Gorbachev created even among his nation's most elite spies would not last. Soon the reforms began
to stall, and the optimism about the new Soviet leader began
to turn into cynicism.

And the reason that the cynics had grown so quickly in
number, even within the ranks of the GRU and the KGB, was
partly attributable to another disaster Gorbachev had inher-
ited, one that was playing out not far from the theater where
Vyacheslav Baranov was posted in the late eighties, the increasingly disastrous war in Afghanistan.

Baranov, once posted abroad, had made it his habit to read
and listen to Western news reports, increasingly so, he says, as
the time wore on. And he knew, both from those reports as
well as from the gossip within the GRU and from Soviet military officers posted in the embassy, that the propaganda
about the war coming from Moscow was blatantly dishonest.
He had befriended a man in the embassy, a military officer
who had been stationed in neighboring Pakistan, which the
Americans were using as a staging ground to run guns to the
mujahedin fighting against the Soviet invaders. This officer,
whom Baranov only identifies as "Volodya," was scathingly
critical of the war effort. He said the young men who were
being sent to war in Afghanistan were, increasingly, poorly
trained, because the military brass had come to realize it
was a quagmire on which their best troops should not be
wasted. But that of course only made it more of a quagmire.

Baranov was appalled by these accounts—and increasingly angered when he read and heard the fiction Moscow peddled. He was also deeply discouraged by the gathering reaction against Gorbachev's policies of "openness" back in Moscow. Particularly shocking to him, he would recall later, was the "humiliation" of human rights advocate Andrei Sakharov— "one of the most honest and dignified people on earth"—at a party congress in the summer of 1989.

By October, Baranov had made a decision. After another volleyball game at the Soviet Mission, Baranov was escorting Brad to the front gate, when he asked "in a low voice" whether the invitation Brad had extended a while back was still open. Brad stiffened, seemed for a moment taken aback, then gathered himself. He said yes, it was, and asked if Baranov still had the card he had given him with his phone number on it. Baranov did, and the two men agreed that Baranov would call him at home within the next day or two. Upon leaving, an elated Brad bolted straight to the home of the CIA's Dhaka station chief, a veteran named Vince, to tell him what had happened.

Baranov was close to making a fateful choice. His own country, bogged down in a terrible war in Afghanistan and enmeshed in a growing economic and political crisis at home, was no place for his young family. He would call the American after all. There were serious things to talk about.

CHAPTER 7

THE SLIPPERY SLOPE

Brad had been surprised by Baranov's response. Months had passed since his initial approach, and he had concluded nothing was going to come of it. It had been, from the American's perspective, a relatively routine probe. No one at the CIA had a particular inkling that Baranov might be ripe for recruiting. He was simply another target, albeit an attractive one—an up-and-coming GRU officer—and at the time Vince, the station chief in Dhaka, was pushing his field agents to make contacts aggressively, even if they were unlikely to pay off.

Baranov did not wait long to follow up. The next day, after work, he walked to a restaurant near the Soviet compound and placed the call to Brad. They agreed to meet the next day, but Baranov was mindful that he could not be gone long from the compound. Even a GRU agent's comings and goings were noted by the security guards, and a long, unexplained absence would draw attention.

They settled on a meeting near a restaurant in a central market area known as Gulshan, not far from where Brad lived. Baranov drove his Toyota Corolla to within about a half mile of the market and left it on a narrow, darkened street. He then walked the rest of the way to the appointed spot for the meeting.

Right on schedule, Brad turned the corner in his Nissan and stopped the car. Baranov got in and closed the door. Brad gunned the engine, streaking down a small darkened alley.

He asked at once whether there was "anything I can do for you," and suddenly Baranov realized Brad might be under the impression that he wanted to close the deal then and there. But recruitment was usually a delicate dance. Sometimes agents, as Aldrich Ames had, just threw themselves at the enemy, usually out of desperation for money. But except for those cases, it took time, almost like a traditional courtship. It took a while to get engaged, and Baranov looked upon this as more of a first date.

"Not so fast, Brad," he said to the CIA agent.

Baranov was nervous, more nervous than he had expected to be. But as Brad drove along, headed for his house and the long-promised dinner, he handed Baranov a mask and told him to put it on. It was a big rubber Halloween mask with thick white hair, a big nose, and glasses. Even under the circumstances Baranov thought this faintly comical, and he assumed Brad was joking. It was pitch-dark, after all, and he was unlikely to be recognized.

But Brad was serious, so Baranov dutifully put the mask

on, and within about fifteen minutes they drove up to Brad's house. As he entered the house Baranov concedes he had some second thoughts. "Why am I bothering with this?" he asked himself.

Brad introduced him to his wife, who had prepared dinner for them. She then left the two men in a sitting room off the main living room, where they chatted idly. Baranov, after his early nervousness, found it relatively easy to talk to Brad. And Baranov was curious about the United States, that was clear. He asked several questions about what life was like for Brad growing up.

That he had other things on his mind also became clear. At one point in the conversation, Baranov asked Brad what Americans thought about the Soviet involvement in Afghanistan. This quickly changed the tenor of the conversation, for it gave Brad a chance to probe Baranov's own thoughts in return.

Brad said he felt a lot of Americans thought the Vietnam analogy was apt. And he added that the right wing of the party of the American president, Ronald Reagan, felt very strongly that the United States should do all it could to see to it that the Soviets did get bogged down. He added that his agency, the CIA, had viewed its own role there as a great success so far. That the fact that the war was ongoing, that the mujahedin continued to put up a bloody resistance against the occupying Soviet forces, emboldened the people in Washington to direct even more funding to the Afghan fighters.

Then Baranov said something that struck Brad, something unexpected from a GRU officer. He said, "You are probably right to be emboldened. Things are not going well there. It is a mess."

Brad noted the comment and filed it away. The outburst had been unexpectedly blunt. He would go back to his embassy that day with very different thoughts about Vyacheslav Baranov than those he arrived with. This might not turn out to be an ordinary pass after all, he later told his station chief. The guy seems pissed off, and he seems curious about the United States. He also said things about his own government that were critical, things Soviet spies don't often say in front of foreigners. Something was up, he thought.

The conversation drifted then from one subject to another aimlessly, until Baranov brought up one he was passionate about—aviation. He talked about his days as a flyer, how thrilling it was to pilot a MIG fighter jet. It was at this point during the evening, Baranov later recalled, that he deliberately sent the American a signal, one that Brad could not miss. He steered the conversation to a discussion of KAL 007, the airliner that in 1983 had been shot down by a Soviet fighter jet over the Sea of Okhotsk, having briefly strayed into Soviet airspace. Two hundred sixty-nine people had been killed. The Soviets had never admitted that the black box from the airliner had ever been recovered, something at the time U.S. intelligence was very interested in. Baranov told Brad that it had been. He didn't tell him how he knew this, other than saying he had heard it from a friend in "aviation circles" back in Moscow. He didn't tell Brad that he, Baranov, had been a member of a small circle of GRU officers who were monitoring the search for the black box, and that he had been on duty the morning of October 22, 1983, more than a month after the plane had been shot down, when the GRU's sea detail in the Far East cabled back that the box had, in fact, been found.

Brad, Baranov recalled later, "was visibly impressed" by this information. He had not expected his guest to offer up information on such a sensitive subject at what the CIA operative thought was still the getting-to-know-you phase of the relationship. Brad did not pursue the subject further that evening. He would come back to it later. But it only strengthened his conviction that Baranov was seriously disgruntled, and seriously thinking of playing ball with the CIA.

The dinner ended and the two men left the house and got into Brad's car. Baranov again put on his mask. As Brad drove toward where Baranov had left his car, he proposed another meeting soon, in just five days. It would again be at Brad's house, and he would again pick Baranov up at a designated spot. It was clear, Baranov recalled, that the CIA "was going to use those five days to have some very serious discussions among themselves." Before he got out of Brad's car, Baranov agreed to the meeting. Fifteen minutes later he was back home, having been gone for about an hour and forty-five minutes. He was sure he went unnoticed, and no one ever questioned him about it.

During the drive back to his apartment, Baranov wondered for the first time what it would be like to spy for another country. By passing along the information about KAL 007 he had crossed a line that night. He had not yet decided to betray his own country, but now he was thinking very seriously about it. He thought, if he were really going to do this, that he would immediately have to get from the Americans a detailed plan for the resettlement of him and his family in the United States, should they have to flee in a hurry. That was going to be his first demand.

He wondered what it would be like to live in the United States. He had two young daughters now, and he doted on them. And he found himself thinking about them as Brad had talked about his childhood; for the first time in his life, he wondered whether they might be better off growing up somewhere other than the Soviet Union or Dhaka, Bangladesh.

There were two ways, if he really wanted to think about it, that he and his daughters could get to the United States. One was for him to be posted there and see what it was like. Or he could commit the high crime of treason—usually punishable in the Soviet Union by a bullet to the back of the head—and spy for the United States, hoping to settle there eventually in CIA-funded comfort.

This was more than a daydream now. He had not in the past thought about spying for the Americans, but now he was on the edge. He had agreed to meet with his new American friend again, and he knew Brad wasn't inviting him for a volleyball game this time.

Dhaka was Baranov's first assignment as a field agent, and he had arrived relatively gung ho. He was never a cheerleader for the system. He was far too rational and coolly intelligent for that. He could see its flaws, and he learned increasingly about how glaring they were compared to the West. Still, he was at the heart of defending that system, first as a military officer, then as an agent for the feared GRU. Yet now, nearly three years into his stint, the CIA was flirting with him—and he was letting it happen.

In recalling this period, Baranov would later talk about how "discouraged" he was becoming by the system he served. The novelty of living abroad had worn off for his wife and family, and they had headed back to Moscow when Baranov had been in the country for three years. That, normally, would have been the end of his time there (three years being the normal tour of duty for a first assignment abroad in the GRU). But Alekseyev, the *rezident*, had told him a few months before Tanya was planning to leave that Moscow could not find an adequate replacement for him and that his tour was going to be extended, perhaps by as much as another year. Baranov was deeply depressed by this. He was dead tired, as he would later put it, and his gloom only deepened when the strong-willed Tatyana insisted on going back anyway. (Baranov would later remark ruefully that he would have avoided "all of the problems that were to come if only my tour had ended on schedule.")

In the five days that he had before his next meeting with Brad, he went for long evening walks. He needed time to think, to think clearly. And not surprisingly, those thoughts would often revolve around the CIA's obvious interest in him—and his interest in them. He began to turn over in his brain the idea of treason.

* * *

At the CIA station in Dhaka, the pursuit of Vyacheslav Baranov was now priority number one. Brad had proposed to meet
in five days for a reason. These were romances, these efforts to
recruit spies, and just as you would never stop calling a woman
you were interested in, neither would you stop contacting
someone you thought you could turn. Baranov was clearly interested, and just how interested was soon to become very
clear. Under these circumstances, you didn't wait.

Five nights later, Brad picked Vyacheslav Baranov up at the
prearranged spot, different from the first one, in the market
section of town, but not that far from it. Baranov again slipped
the mask on, and the two traveled, mostly in silence, through
the streets of Dhaka. As they approached the gate to Brad's
house, which like many in the diplomatic district was surrounded by a high brick wall, Brad honked his horn. A gate-
keeper, a *chokidar,* as the Bangladeshis called him, looked out,
saw it was Brad, and opened the gate.

Once they were inside the house, Baranov could see that
the American was all business. His wife was nowhere to be
seen. But there was another man present, and Baranov recognized him. His name was "Vince," the CIA station chief in
Dhaka. This, indeed, was not going to be a social call.

The three men sat in Brad's den. Vince started the conversation by inquiring about Baranov's family, asking whether
they were still in Dhaka. Baranov said no, they had returned to
Moscow several months earlier—when he had been scheduled

to leave. Vince asked how much longer Baranov would be in Bangladesh. Baranov said it would be just a few more months, that he had been promised his tour was not going to be prolonged more than one full year.

Vince then cut straight to the point. The Americans had plainly decided there was no point in subtlety with Baranov. He had made himself available. Indeed, after declining Brad's original dinner invitation after the first volleyball game, he had *initiated* the second meeting and had readily agreed to this one, the third. Now the task at hand was the details of treason. Was Baranov willing, at what price, toward what ends? Brad said little during the meeting. It was Vince who was laying out the terms and trying to close the sale.

Years later, Baranov would have a hard time recalling just what was going through his mind as this conversation unfolded. It was a meeting that would profoundly affect the rest of his life in ways he could not then imagine. He was there, listening, and that by itself meant he was interested. More than that, he had convinced himself to betray, if not his country, then at least the "system" that he said he despised.

But there was, at the same time, a reluctance, a deep ambivalence about what he was in the process of doing. Baranov stressed that the safety and security of his family was paramount. He was increasingly pessimistic about how things were going in the Soviet Union. Gorbachev was failing and Baranov was sure that hardliners were plotting a comeback. He wanted an escape plan; he wanted assurances that the U.S. government would pay to relocate him and his family, should it come to that. There was then great ferment in what used to be called the Soviet bloc. The Communist leadership in Poland was under severe pressure from the Lech Walesa–led trade unionists. Demonstrations had begun in Prague in Czechoslovakia. Baranov viewed all this pessimistically. The people who paid his salary would not let anything come of this, he believed. (And however inaccurate history proved that judgment to be, it was the same position held by leaders across the NATO alliance at precisely the same time. If you had looked anyone in the eye in late 1988 and said that in two years time the Berlin Wall would fall, the Soviet bloc would be history, and the Soviet Union was just two years from collapse, you would not have held a position in government long— not in Washington, not in London, not in Bonn.)

Vince said he understood, and he then used a phrase that would stick with Baranov for a long time to come. He said if Baranov agreed to spy for the United States, he would be entitled to the "full protection of the U.S. government."

That was what Baranov wanted to hear. He was impressed by the phrase but still was not quite ready to sign on the dotted line. He then asked a question that he would, years later, concede was a big mistake, "a stupid thing to say." He looked at Vince and asked, if upon relocation to the United States, "what if I refuse to be debriefed?"

Vince couldn't quite believe what he had heard. An agency official would later describe this as the equivalent of a woman, about to be engaged, blithely asking her husband to be if "sex had to be part of the deal." For a professional of Baranov's caliber to say such a thing, under the circumstances, was flabbergasting.

And it would, not too far down the road, come to haunt him.

Vince's demeanor turned icy. "If you refuse to be debriefed," he said, glaring at Baranov, "you will be treated as an illegal refugee upon arrival in the United States. You will get no help from the U.S. government." The CIA, he added acidly, is "not a travel agency."

Baranov would later say his question simply betrayed his ambivalence about the profound decision he was about to make. He realized he had made a mistake as soon as he saw how angrily Vince responded. He backpedaled, said of course he understood. He then paused for a long while, then finally said, "Okay, gentlemen, we have an understanding."

Having crossed the threshold, the rest of the meeting was "mostly a fog" to Baranov, he said later. They would discuss the mechanics of their next meeting, which, because his time in Dhaka was growing relatively short, was an important one. Among other things, they were to hash out the methods and timing of his communication with the agency once he arrived back in Moscow. Once that was done, the meeting ended.

The CIA had their man. His code name was to be "Agent Tony." He had been in Brad's house nearly two hours, and Baranov told his hosts he had better be heading back, lest his late return to the mission raise suspicion. When he left that evening, he was the highest-ranking Soviet recruit since Dmitry Polyakov—the famed Agent Top Hat—who had agreed to spy for Washington in the mid-eighties. And he left believing that he took with him the "full protection of the United States government."

CHAPTER 8

TESTING GROUND

When "Agent Tony" was recruited, there was a strange combination of elation and unease at the CIA station in Dhaka. Baranov was a prize catch, a high-flying officer well on his way to the GRU's upper echelons. As Vince later put it, "Guys like that don't come across the transom too often."

The unease was rooted in one simple question. Had Baranov's recruitment been *too* easy? Was it possible that Baranov was a dangle, a double agent sent by the Soviets to feed the agency disinformation? Some in the station thought it possible. Vince, in fact, couldn't get Baranov's question—"What if I refuse to be debriefed?"—out of his head. It was also true that Baranov was pretty close to what spies call a "gangplank" walk-in. He had made himself available, had signed on quickly, and had done so just before he was to be reassigned to headquarters. In the past that pattern had often been bad news. The

KGB in particular had used it to run double agents against the CIA in Moscow. They could feed disinformation through their agent and see how and where the agency operated on enemy territory.

Brad didn't share those concerns. He felt, and argued strongly to his superiors, that some agents are recruited easily because they are ready to turn. "They've already made up their minds and are just waiting for the invitation," as one agency veteran would later put it.

The suspicion would follow Baranov back to Moscow when his tour of duty in Dhaka ended. He could not know it, but he had signed on with Langley during one of the worst periods in the agency's less than glorious history. Starting as early as 1986, Soviet agents, both in Moscow and in the United States, who had agreed to become CIA "assets" had begun to disappear—their betrayal discovered by their masters—and would continue to do so over the next several years at a horrifying rate. In time most of these disappearances would be traced to Aldrich Ames. But in 1989, when the damage he did was escalating rapidly, there was at the agency a growing sense of paranoia, particularly in the so-called Soviet–Near East division, the most important section of the agency during the Cold War.

Baranov was potentially a prized new informant. The agency was keenly interested in seeing what he could deliver, particularly senior officials back at Langley, who were much more suspicious than the Dhaka station about any Soviet asset, especially one whose recruitment had been so relatively easy.

In the spying game, a new recruit is asked to prove his bona fides, to deliver a piece of information sufficiently sensitive that it will convince his handlers that he is the real deal, and not a double agent. Baranov had mistakenly believed that his telling Brad early on about the Korean airliner showed that he was serious. And, in fact, that piece of information did impress the Dhaka station, as well as a lot of folks back in Washington. At the time of the incident, the Reagan administration had made full use of it for propaganda purposes, exhibit number one, back then, that the Soviet Union really was an "evil empire." But six years later, the fact was no one had all the details as to what, exactly, had happened. Both Washington and Seoul remained keenly interested in the contents of the black box, and the fact that Moscow had it meant they could try to find out what was on it.

One more meeting remained with his new handlers in Dhaka before Baranov was to head back to Moscow. They had worked out a series of signals, chalk marks left on a building about a mile and a half from the Soviet embassy, that would let each side know a meeting was on. Baranov saw the signal one day just about a month before he was to depart, and a few days later he met Brad and Vince for the last time.

At this meeting, they asked more questions about the black box, including specifics about what was on it. Baranov says he answered as best as he could, but wasn't sure whether any of the details he could provide were of any value at that point. Then Brad asked him flatly whether he had access to the cable traffic headed in and out of the GRU station in Dhaka. Bara-

nov said no, and Vince looked at him skeptically. In fact, Baranov would later explain, the answer was "mostly true—but not
100 percent true."

Standard operating procedure for any GRU station had it
that a cipher clerk be present when all dispatches were sent off
for Moscow. A cipher clerk had to be present, moreover, if any
agent wanted to change the contents of a cable he was sending. The point of this was security—to prevent men like Baranov from copying cables and giving them to men like Brad.

In practice, however, the system wasn't unbeatable. Baranov's relative success in Dhaka—the recruitment of "Ahmed,"
who had been included into the GRU's international network
of agents on the payroll—had made him a figure of respect
within the *rezidentura*. He had befriended the cipher clerk,
who would not infrequently leave the communications room
to attend to other matters when Baranov was transmitting or
editing material headed for Moscow. In short, Baranov could
have provided some cables had he been so inclined, but it
would have been risky. If the cipher clerk ever spotted him
copying cables, which was strictly against regulations, Baranov
would have been in trouble.

Rebuffed on the cables, Brad then asked if they could get
a copy of Baranov's "log book," a diary of sorts that included
his daily activities, future tasks as assigned by Moscow Center,
and a list of GRU sources in Dhaka. Baranov, to Brad's irrita-
tion, again said no. Why not? Brad asked. Baranov dissembled.
He had not been able to accomplish much in his tour, he said.
The sources he had were not so important.

We can be the judge of that, Brad responded. Baranov again waved him off, asking Brad, in effect, to let him start his work once he got to Moscow. He would later say to me that this again simply reflected his ambivalence about the venture he had signed on for, that it was too soon to turn over his log book and "cause so much damage."

Whether this was true or not, it put the Americans in a dilemma. Their prized colonel was not very forthcoming, at least not right out of the gate. Beyond KAL 007 he had offered nothing of much value in Dhaka. They had to decide, quickly, whether they thought Baranov was real or whether he was a dangle.

Brad, despite not getting the information he had sought, continued to believe Baranov was a genuine asset. Vince, his boss, was less convinced but was willing to give him more time to prove it. At the end of the meeting Vince handed Baranov $2,500 in cash and told him there would be more coming.

As they drove back to the embassy they were content enough with what they had pulled off. Baranov was coming to the end of his Dhaka tour and would be heading back to Moscow. He was already a full colonel, having been promoted after his successful recruitment of "Ahmed." In Moscow he would be in on a lot of the GRU's secrets—secrets the CIA would be very interested in. A recruit like this, for an agent like Brad, could make a career, and it certainly wasn't going to hurt Vince's reputation as a station chief either. If, that is, Baranov proved to be the real thing. And that, they decided, was something the CIA's officers in

Moscow could figure out quickly enough. If he produced, fine. If not, they would cut him off.

Baranov would later recall that for him, turning over the KAL 007 information was more important than merely providing good gossip for the boys back at Langley. He remembered reading after the crash a Soviet military report about the debris that had been recovered after the plane went down. "Kids clothes, dolls, shoes. My daughter was four years old at the time, and I was shocked by this incident, and by the way our government lied about it. From that point on really my resentment toward the system had started to grow."

It had been six years since then. It was the fall of 1989. The Berlin Wall, astonishingly, came down in November, and the other governments in the East bloc also toppled like dominoes: Czechoslovakia, Poland, Hungary—all experienced "velvet revolutions": communist regimes collapsing while Moscow, and Mikhail Gorbachev, looked on and did nothing.

This was a time of extraordinary hope as millions of people got their first taste of political freedom. But Baranov, strangely, did not share in that hope. While he watched in wonderment and quietly applauded the events in Eastern Europe, he believed nothing of the sort would ever happen in his own country. As he had told Vince in Dhaka, he feared a reactionary coup in Moscow would depose Gorbachev and that the hardliners would be back in charge. He said that if this happened, he wanted the United States to get him out—to devise a plan to relocate him and his family to the United States. At his last meeting in Dhaka, far from wondering whether he would have to be debriefed, he told Vince, "I will tell you everything that I know about the GRU, about the Soviet military, about anything you want to ask me about."

Vince was somewhat taken aback by his fatalism. He asked whether he had any information to back up his fear of a coup. No, Baranov said, it was just a foreboding.[*]

Vince assured him that arrangements would be made for his and his family's safety in the event the worst happened. Alone and depressed, Baranov was relieved to hear Vince's commitment. He could not shake the dark feelings he had even as East European governments tottered. He was on one hand anxious to return to Moscow to be with his family and also acutely aware of how awful things had become economically at home. Even as a full GRU colonel, their lifestyle in Dhaka was better than it was going to be in Moscow. Nonetheless, he knew his reassignment was coming up. And he would spend the rest of his days in Dhaka simply passing time, waiting for his orders, which would come soon enough. It was time to go home.

---

[*]An accurate foreboding, as events less than two years later would prove, though of course the coup against Gorbachev would mercifully fail and lead to Boris Yeltsin's rise to power in the new Russia.

CHAPTER 9

TO THE MOSCOW STATION

On November 6, 1989, Vyacheslav Baranov left Dhaka for his new assignment back in Moscow. With a cover job in the Soviet Foreign Trade Ministry, he was assigned to what was known as the First Separate Directorate of the GRU, whose main responsibility was to recruit foreigners as informants. He was glad to be reunited with his family, and had no regrets about his new role as a prized CIA spy. The worsening economic conditions only deepened his contempt for the system he had served for years. The lines in stores got longer as the shelves grew barer.

Vince, head of station in Dhaka, fought hard to convince agency headquarters in Langley that Baranov was the genuine article, a spy and not a double agent. But doubts lingered, and indeed as the months passed, actually grew, as the Ames body count mounted.

Because there were doubts in Langley, they were shared, to some extent, at the agency's station in Moscow. Baranov's handler was Deputy Chief of Station Mike. Mike had been in Moscow for two years before Baranov arrived, and was nearing the end of his tour of duty there. It had not been a pleasant one, despite the arrival of a prized GRU colonel as the agency's newest recruit. As the agency's network of spies got rolled up and liquidated by the KGB, paranoia in the Moscow station grew. It would eventually get to the point, as one agent later put it, "where we had almost primal fear to leave the embassy." Something was going seriously wrong, and one obvious possibility was that the Soviets had a very well-placed mole. One by one, spies within Russia (and abroad) were disappearing.

This was Ames's handiwork, but it would take another four years before a devastated agency official would go to the FBI in Washington and confess "we have blood on our hands," thus kick-starting the investigation that would lead to Ames's arrest.

Before leaving Dhaka, Baranov had worked out at his last meeting with Vince, an elaborate scheme by which his first contact in Moscow would be initiated. Vince had told him the agency wanted him to lie low for the first six months upon his return. Act as if it's business as usual and don't do anything to draw attention to yourself. Act as if you're happy to be back. The two then went over the plan by which he would initiate contact after the six-month interval, and here Baranov had taken the initiative. He proposed that he scribble a phone number in a phone booth directly in front of the central post office in Moscow, at a heavily trafficked square called

Kirovskaya. It would be a specific phone number, not just an "X" or some other kind of mark. As he explained it to Vince, this would ensure safety against KGB "sweep teams," which were routinely dispatched through Moscow looking for suspicious signs or markings on buildings—not to mention the people who might make them. Baranov told Vince that a phone number in a public phone booth would be safer than an "X" marked on some building somewhere. Vince agreed, and Baranov assumed that this information had been passed on to the Moscow station and approved there as well.

He assumed incorrectly. What Baranov thought was a safe, relatively simple plan to initiate contact had become something of a controversy within the embassy in Moscow. The agency liked signals that could be seen easily from a car, thus avoiding any risk that an agent could be arrested in a setup. Baranov's phone-booth scheme only reinforced the suspicions of those in the agency Moscow station that Baranov might be a dangle. And if he was, perhaps the phone-booth scheme *was* a setup, intended to lure one of Baranov's handlers into a trap.

Mike had some sympathy for these arguments, but decided that Baranov was too important an asset to waste if he was genuine. Mike's solution: For an assignment that would normally have been given a more junior agent in the station, he would himself go to the booth to see if there was a signal. He had, he reasoned, only about a month to go on his Moscow assignment, so if he was arrested and thrown out of the country, it was, as he put it to one of his colleagues, "no big deal."

Beginning in June 1990, Mike began making swings by the

Kirovskaya phone booth to check for Baranov's number. On June 15, Baranov left his office at the Trade Ministry in Moscow, made the fifteen-minute journey over to the phone booth, and left the number. A day later, Mike, making his fourth pass by the booth, spotted it.

Phase two of the plan called for the meeting to take place a few days after the signal was left. And again, it was Baranov who had made the suggestion, accepted by Vince in Dhaka, as to where and how the meeting would take place. On the platform at a commuter train station, called Youza, next to a lovely, thickly wooded park called Sokolniki, Baranov would wait for his agency contact (he had been given pictures of his handlers, and vice versa). Upon making eye contact, the two would disappear into the woods and rendezvous five minutes later, assuming both concluded that they were not under surveillance.

Members of the agency staff in Moscow again raised objections. Why were they agreeing to a plan put forth by the agent, when they were supposed to be running *him*? Wasn't there an enormous risk that this was going to be a setup? Mike again made the decision that the meeting would go off as planned, and that he would attend.

On June 20, Baranov went to the platform at Youza station, and watched and waited. For three hours he looked for Mike. But CIA agents could hardly roam about Moscow unmolested. They were tailed aggressively by KGB counterintelligence units each time they left the embassy compound. For seven and a half hours that day, Mike drove around Moscow trying desperately to lose his tail. He failed.

Baranov was not unduly alarmed. He knew how effective his brethren in the KGB were in harassing foreign intelligence agents, and it was more than plausible that Mike had a good reason for not showing up. As for him, he had been out of the office on a business meeting, he had said, but to be gone for too long would draw unwanted attention. So he left, knowing that was the nature of the game. It was on to round two.

On July 11, having left the signal in the phone booth again days earlier, Baranov again went to the Youza train platform, and this time Mike made it, too. A few minutes later, with no one around in the heavy woods, agent and handler met for the first time. After exchanging brief pleasantries, Mike handed him a package. In it was a plan of proposed meeting dates, locations for dead letter drops, and 2,000 rubles (about $100) in cash so Baranov could buy a shortwave radio with which he could receive agency transmissions on specified dates. It was the only time Baranov and Mike would meet.

The meeting lasted just a few minutes. Baranov quickly went back to his office at the Trade Ministry, pretended to do paperwork for a while, and then left early for home, explaining to a co-worker that one of his daughters had fallen ill and he needed to go to a drugstore for some medicine.

At home, Baranov opened the package Mike had given him, and was surprised not by what it contained, but by what it didn't. To his bewilderment, the plan of action he received did not contain two of what Baranov would later describe to me as "the most basic, canonic elements" of professional trade-craft in the spying game: "the mechanism for reestablishing lost contact, and an emergency signal for both sides."

He was also astonished to find that the instructions said he was to leave signals in an area near the Donskoy Monastery along the Moscow River. The monastery was famous for its serene beauty and a cemetery where many famous Russians were buried, but to spies in the Soviet Union it was famous for another reason: it was one of the most heavily patrolled areas by KGB counterintelligence units. "Notoriously so," Baranov said later.

This was the entire reason, he thought to himself, that *he* had suggested the plans for the initial meetings to Vince in Dhaka. Moscow was his home turf, and as he put it, "I knew it better than any American." He also knew the KGB's tactics better than the Americans, and was stunned when he saw the proposed location for signals. That, combined with the absence of a plan for reestablishing lost contact and a procedure to deal with an emergency, left him unsettled. He had specifically told Vince that there might be circumstances in which he and his family would want to be whisked out of Moscow in a hurry, and these "plans" took no account of that.

As a professional spy, he had no illusions that he was dealing with James Bond–like supermen. But these, in his mind, were matters of basic competence, like a carpenter being able to drive a nail into a piece of wood. He wondered what the agency men could possibly have been thinking. There was no way to find out, not anytime soon anyway. He was in now, he was the CIA's new Joe, the great new recruit, and he had to stick by the plan they had provided. Vyacheslav Baranov's troubles with his new employer had only just begun.

CHAPTER 10

HOME ALONE

In July, shortly after Mike's tour in Moscow ended, Baranov, as per the instructions given him in Dhaka, bought a short-wave radio, a used Sony that he got from a friend for 1,000 rubles. Over the next month, he received several transmissions from the CIA station, but they were all tests, containing no "operational" instructions. Then, for the next three months, there was radio silence. No communication whatsoever. For nearly a year now, the CIA's prized recruit had been back in Moscow, on the payroll, and there had been all of one meeting.

Baranov of course could not know of the increasing fear that was gripping the CIA station in Moscow. By late 1990 it was obvious to all that there was a security breach somewhere, but no one knew where or in what form. The paranoia further limited the actions and travels of the agency's Moscow agents.

Indeed, at times it brought on utter paralysis. Recruitment of new agents virtually stopped on orders from Langley for obvious reasons. If your existing network is getting rolled up, it doesn't make much sense to go out and get new agents who are going to be betrayed. At the same time, those officials at Langley who were wary of Baranov continued to voice their skepticism. That had a dramatic impact on how he was "handled" by Moscow station.

Bewildered by the lack of contact from his new friends, Baranov on four separate occasions left signals on walls in different Moscow neighborhoods. When he needed to make contact, he had been told in his original instructions, write a Cyrillic "G" at any of four locations. On November 15, Baranov walked to a location on Pluschika Street in a residential neighborhood and again scrawled a "G." That night, as he had the previous three times, he would listen to his shortwave after his family had gone to bed, hoping to hear a return signal indicating his message had been received. But the silence continued.

The contingency plan, if the signs on the walls were not heeded, was a dead-letter drop of a coded message, telling his handlers that he needed to meet urgently. Such a drop, according to the instructions he received in Dhaka, was to take place exactly three days after the last signal had been placed on the wall. So just before Christmas of 1990, Baranov walked late one evening into a yard adjacent to a garage where cars owned by foreign embassies in Moscow were serviced, one of the prearranged drop sites. There was a large garbage cart there, and

Baranov left his package just behind it, underneath two concrete blocks that were covered by a thin piece of sheet metal. Surely, he thought, as he drove back home that night, the agency would see this and respond. There could be no excuse not to. Basic tradecraft in the spying game said a dead drop had to be retrieved and responded to, at the least with a signal that the message was received.

For two days Baranov waited. Another day passed, and still no response from the agency. Baranov was beside himself. He couldn't fathom what was going on. Had Dhaka been a dream? Had he really signed on with the CIA? What was going on here?

Baranov considered himself a consummate professional, a spy who had learned his lessons well and hewed to them faithfully. But the mystery of what was going on now, the feeling of being left high and dry, finally overwhelmed his professionalism. He was so agitated by the lack of communication from his handlers that he broke a cardinal rule. On the evening of December 28, 1990, he ventured back into the yard next to the garage to have a look at the dead-drop site again. This was hugely risky. He knew how persistent the KGB counterintelligence units were, how aggressively they tailed the Americans, and in particular how much effort they put into trying to locate their dead-drop sites. Going back to a drop site for a spy is, under most circumstances, a brainless act for exactly that reason. If the KGB happens to know it's a site that is used, then the possibility of being seen is enormous.

Baranov went anyway, and creeping there, alone as far as he could tell, he was astonished when he saw the package; lying exactly where he had put it. It had not been moved an inch. No one had picked it up. Stunned, he glanced around again to make sure he hadn't been followed. He waited for several minutes, holding himself as still as he possibly could, and listened for any sound that might indicate that he had company. There was nothing.

He darted out from behind a tree and grabbed the package, tucked it under his arm, and quickly left, again checking to make sure that no one was around. He got in his car and drove home, amazed at what he had just done, and, as he felt, had to do.

Spying can be a very lonely existence. Baranov, of course, had told no one about his betrayal, not his wife, not his closest friends. The only people who knew were those who had recruited him, and now it was as if they did not exist. They were ghosts who had disappeared into the Moscow winter.

Baranov ran through all the possibilities of what could be going wrong: did the Americans not trust him? Did they think he was a double agent? He discounted that. Mike had shown up that summer, after all, and Baranov, as far as he knew, had proven his bona fides. The possibility that there was a security breach within the agency is something he also considered, that for some reason agents were not doing what they are supposed to do. But would that account for both the lack of radio communication *and* the fact that a critical dead drop had been ignored? The fact was he could not know what was going on inside the embassy—what they were thinking, what they were doing. It was driving him crazy.

At the Academy, he would say later, referring to his GRU

training, "We were told that the agent must be warned and saved at any cost (if there is a problem) because he risks more than the intelligence officer—even if there are suspicions about the agent." In the GRU, to cut off an agent, to leave him to his own wits, required hard evidence of "his rottenness." But the agency had no evidence that Baranov was rotten, only their own fears. It was in one of the most hideous periods of its history, and those fears were now starting to dictate its actions. Having recruited Baranov, it had now effectively dropped him, at least for the time being.

After the appalling experience with the dead-letter drop, Baranov did not attempt a second. Too risky, he thought. For more than two months, he continued to listen to his radio at the prescribed times, hoping desperately for a signal. Finally, in April, he gave up.

Furious and, as he said, living by his wits, Baranov was continuing his cover work for the Foreign Trade Ministry in Moscow. And one month later, the kind of random event that can disrupt the best-laid plans of spies and men, occurred, and it only deepened Baranov's misery. He had taken to keeping the shortwave radio in the trunk of his car, fearful that his wife or one of his children might happen on it accidentally at home. In late May, he discovered one morning that the trunk had been broken into, and the radio stolen.

The timing of this would turn out to be excruciating. The CIA's Moscow station, in June, would again attempt to overcome Langley's skepticism about Baranov, and this time did so successfully. They were given the go-ahead to try to reestablish contact with him, and they did. Over the next three months, the agency sent out thirty urgent signals over the radio, with one message: reestablish contact with us. Each of the messages contained details of proposed meeting sites and signals he was to send in return, accepting or postponing a meeting.

Vyacheslav Baranov never received any of those messages. But someone else, he would later learn, did.

Furious about the dead drop and then the absence of any radio communication, he never bought another shortwave after the theft. In his own mind, he would recall later, he was convinced "my association with the agency had been terminated."

CHAPTER 11

VIENNA BOUND

In the middle of June 1991, Baranov made one last, despairing attempt to contact his agency handlers. He again risked surveillance by walking to Pluschika Street and leaving another signal—the red "G" that the Dhaka instructions called for. After having had his radio stolen, and never having received anything other than test messages from the embassy, he never bought another one, and thus could not know that on the airwaves now were repeated pleas for him to make contact back. But no one from the agency was checking Pluschika Street anymore—that would become clear. For several days after, he checked the site to see if the signal had been answered (with a simple chalk mark in blue). It had not.

Baranov felt he had no way now of contacting the agency, and had given up hope that anyone was trying to reach him. Furious and frustrated, he could do nothing other than carry out his cover assignment for the GRU in the Soviet Foreign Trade Ministry, while also performing his real job—which was to recruit foreigners as informers for Soviet military intelligence.

In truth, and for obvious reasons, his heart was not in either task, but particularly the latter. Nonetheless, he knew he risked suspicion if he did nothing. As best he could, Baranov acted as if nothing was amiss. Over the next several months, along with colleagues from the ministry, he helped set up businesses, one for the export of children's toys to western Europe, and one exporting diamonds mined in Siberia. But the spying side of his work flagged, and Baranov could only be relieved that his masters in the GRU evinced no great concern about it. He attributed that to the fact that he was relatively new to the assignment back in Moscow and they were smart enough to be patient with him. How wrong a conclusion this would turn out to be.

Baranov's anger and confusion did not dissipate, as the agency's silence continued. But back at the U.S. Embassy, and in Langley, it was the CIA that was confused, as Baranov failed to respond to all the radio messages. Mike, who still believed he was the real thing, felt that there must be sound reasons for the lack of response. Perhaps Baranov had had a whiff of KGB counterintelligence surveillance, or perhaps for some reason he felt the radio signals were not secure. Mike counseled patience, and so for three months the signals continued to go out.

By the autumn of 1991, the CIA had given up on Baranov, and he was close to giving up on them. In the instructions that had been given him in Dhaka, there was one set that was meant to signal the need for an urgent meeting if—and only if—Baranov happened to be traveling outside Russia on "business" (in his guise as a foreign trade official). For months he bided his time, hoping to be able to arrange just such a trip, where he would also make one last attempt to meet with a CIA officer.

Finally, in August of 1992, more than a year after his last, failed effort to leave a signal for the agency, Baranov managed to scam a trip abroad. He had found buyers in Vienna interested in the diamond venture, and was going to go to Luxembourg via Vienna in order to register a company in his name, something that he had been told could be done within three days. He did not intend to tell his superiors at the GRU about this trip. He had been thinking vaguely of resigning, and the business potential of the diamond venture was real. If it paid off, it might develop into a full-time job. (And in post–Soviet Russia, it was actually possible for GRU officers to think both of resigning *and* of making money.) That, plus the fact that he was going to try to contact the agency while in Vienna, made Baranov think he'd be better off traveling on a phony passport. He arranged for that through a friend, a former KGB officer, paying $500 for the service rendered. The prospective diamond customers in Vienna arranged for a visa to Austria. Baranov also needed to borrow some money, since it took $2,500 to register a business in Luxembourg then, and he could only put his hands on $1,500. Another friend, named Viktor, agreed to loan him the money.

The evening before he left, he told Tatyana that he was going to Vienna on trade ministry business the next morning, and would be back three days later, on Friday the fourteenth. He left their apartment at about 8:15 the next morning, and hailed a cab to take him to central Moscow, where he met Viktor at the Hotel Beijing to pick up the $1,000. From there Baranov flagged down another car to take him to Sheremetyevo Airport. Sheremetyevo was one of the dreariest airports in the world: poor lighting, cracked green paint falling from the walls, and sullen women in olive green uniforms staffing the customs booths. It was a depressing place to arrive, and one you couldn't be happier to leave. If ever there was an airport that said "police state," it was Sheremetyevo.

But when Vyacheslav Baranov made the drive that morning, he was no longer in a police state. Over the past year, as the painful string of screwups with the agency proceeded, the country that he was ostensibly serving had disappeared. Mikhail Gorbachev had let Eastern Europe go free, and just as Baranov had feared it would, this triggered a coup attempt in August 1993 in his own country. But the KGB generals and others who planned and executed the coup were hapless, and had (among other obvious failings) not counted on the intervention of Moscow party boss Boris Nikolaevich Yeltsin, on Gorbachev's behalf. The image of Yeltsin standing on the tanks in front of what was then the Russian parliament (it had been turned into the Russian White House, home to the prime minister, by the time I arrived in Moscow) became one of the two most enduring symbols of Russia's second revolution.

The other was when masses of people descended upon

Dzherzhinsky Square, home to KGB headquarters, and toppled the giant statue that stood at the center of the square: the
statue of Felix Dzherzhinsky himself, the founding father of
the Soviet Union's secret police.

Baranov, like so many of his countrymen, had been in-
spired by these events, but later would insist he never really believed the changes would stick. Having made the decision to
betray his country, he could not bring himself to believe that
the change toward democracy and something resembling a
market economic system could last. There were too many
powerful people whose entire lives and careers, not to mention
their perks, prestige, and privileges, had come from the state.
They were not going to let that state perish, he believed. Some
of his bosses in the GRU, of course, were among them. If the
first coup plotters were incompetent, the second would know
what they were doing.

Thus, Baranov would later claim never to have had any
second thoughts about what he had done based upon anything
that had happened subsequently in his own country. None.
Baranov had about him, even during the late 1990s, the world-
weary air of the born pessimist, particularly when it came to
his own nation. So as he entered Sheremetyevo that August
morning preparing to board a flight to Vienna, he had no
doubts that he was doing the right thing: trying to make contact one last time with the CIA.

*   *   *

Baranov went to the check-in counter, waited in a long line, handed over a single bag, and got his boarding pass. He then proceeded to customs, about fifty minutes before his scheduled flight. He waited in line for about fifteen minutes, and nothing, as he would later describe the scene, seemed amiss. He got to the counter and presented his documents. The young border guard looked at his papers, then back at him. He paused, looked again, and then looked up and just sat there, neither stamping the passport nor giving it back. Finally he said the visa stamp wasn't visible enough.

At that moment, a uniformed officer moved through the line and was standing next to him. He asked Baranov to step away from the counter and to accompany him. He said they would clear this up quickly and he would make his flight.

Baranov tried to stay calm as he followed the officer down a long corridor, then down a flight of stairs to the arrivals level at Sheremetyevo. Perhaps they just wanted to question him about the business nature of his trip. Or maybe there was some other reason why he was taken out of line. Stay calm, he told himself. Don't give anything away.

Any hope he might have had disappeared soon after he entered a conference room down the stairs.

One uniformed officer sat at the head of a T-shaped desk at the far end of the room. He asked for Baranov's passport and asked who he was. He replied he was a staff member of Machina-Export, the division of the Foreign Trade Ministry that served as his cover. The officer replied, "Who are you really?"

Baranov said he was an officer of the GRU.

Is the GRU leadership aware of your plans to travel abroad? the officer inquired.

Baranov replied truthfully, saying no, it was a private venture, he intended to register a company abroad. The officer paused, then asked, What is the real reason for your trip abroad, Colonel?

At that point, Baranov would later recall, "I began to suspect the worst." He struggled to keep calm as his mind raced. He wondered to himself whether he had done anything in the last years that might have given him away, but he could think of nothing. He had turned over no classified documents, no important state secrets. The one time he had attempted to provide significant information, the Keystone-cops quality of his dealings with the CIA ensured that it had been a bust: in the dead drop that the agency failed to pick up, Baranov had included a list of new GRU field agents, as a sign of his willingness to do business. But no one could know that because no one had ever received it.

For fifteen minutes the officer continued to question him, Baranov insisting all the while that nothing was amiss. Then, another door to the office opened, and two more men walked in, one of whom was in a general's uniform.

At that moment, Baranov knew he was in serious trouble. The general was Gennadi Andreavich Molykov, the chief of military counterintelligence at what had been the KGB (it had been rechristened at the time as the Ministry of Security and would later become the Federal Security Bureau, or FSB).

Molykov told Baranov he was under arrest for violation of

article 64 of the Russian Federation's Criminal Code. Espionage. Baranov was reeling, but he had to find out how much they knew, and calibrate his answers accordingly. What evidence do you have of this? he asked Molykov.

"We have plenty of evidence, Vyacheslav Maximovich." And with that he instructed the GRU colonel to take a seat. As his questioning began, Molykov began to reveal some of that evidence. And as he did, what was left of Baranov's spirits sank. He could not believe what he was hearing.

CHAPTER 12

REVELATION

Baranov would later say he recognized at the time that much depended upon what he said, and didn't say, as this first interrogation proceeded. "The common practice," he said, "is to get the suspect to break right away, and to tell everything." He had to fence with Molykov and his deputy, a man named Karela, until he could figure out as best he could what had prompted the arrest. How much did the KGB men know, and how did they come to know it?

The KGB was filming the interrogation with a camera hidden inside a wall in the room. It would later be shown, edited of course, on a *60 Minutes*–like program glorifying the counterintelligence capabilities of the KGB. The film shows the session proceeding inconclusively for several minutes, until Molykov says, "And what about Dhaka, what took place in Dhaka?"

Baranov shook his head and said he didn't understand. Molykov replied, "Didn't you meet some of our opponents there?"

Baranov would later admit that at the point, a wave of "great unease" swept over him, but he remained composed. "I was still feeling that they didn't have anything concrete, only suspicions." It would do him no good to lie blatantly, however, so Baranov responded that, yes, he had come in contact with some American agents, but that those contacts had been duly reported to the embassy.

And what, the general continued, about the black box?

At first Baranov says he did not even understand the question. Then at once its meaning hit him. Molykov meant the KAL 007 black box. Now, as he would later put it, "It was obvious which way the wind was blowing." On the tape Baranov gets a blank look on his face, and there is a long pause. It was at this moment, as fractured as he was by his arrest, that the professional spy Vyacheslav Maximovich Baranov came to consider the likelihood that there was only one possibility. Someone, somewhere, knew that he had signed on with the CIA, and had told Moscow.

What, possibly, could be a plausible alternative explanation? That KGB counterintelligence, either in Dhaka or in the time he had been back in Moscow, had been so proficient that they had locked onto him in what, in the spying game, amounts to a virtual instant? Could that possibly be true?

Baranov's mind was reeling. As far as he knew at this moment, he was headed for the basement at Lubyanka, KGB headquarters, and possibly a bullet in the back of his head. But at the same time, as he thought of possible explanations, only one really made sense, as a hypothesis at least, and (in terms of what he felt in his gut) as a virtual certainty: there had been a tip-off. From the moment he arrived in Moscow, KGB counterintelligence must have known that he had signed on with the CIA.

In the years that would follow, as Baranov spent time in Perm 35—the prison camp in the Urals that was home, during the Soviet era, to dissidents and other prominent political prisoners—he would consider other possibilities. Since Baranov was one of only about 200 people who knew about the black box, that could have drawn suspicion from the KGB. If the Soviets had been able to intercept American communications from the embassy in Dhaka back to Washington, it is possible they could have traced the KAL 007 information back to him, since he was the only one in the Soviet Embassy there who had access to that information. He thought about this, considered it, but as he would soon learn at his trial in Moscow, it was not the case. He believed he had been betrayed. The question was, by whom?

The videotape of August 11 shows Baranov looking at the photo, then at Molykov, and there is an expression on his face, a blankness and, perhaps strangely, a calmness, that says one thing: he knows the jig is up. However they had gotten onto him, they were onto him. And Baranov was cool enough to know that to deny everything at that point was counterproductive. Indeed, when you think you may likely be shot in the head anyway, but want to try to save yourself, it doesn't make sense to play make-believe. So when Molykov put a picture of Mike in front of him and asked if he was his contact at the CIA's Moscow station, Baranov replied, yes, he was.

The initial interrogation then got very specific: When had he signed on? Who had recruited him? When he met with Mike in Moscow, in the park nearby the train station, what had transpired?

Again, he did not deny anything. Without going into his motives, he told of meeting with Brad in Dhaka, and then with Vince. He told of the instructions he had been given, and of his disbelief when he had seen them: how there was no escape route, no plan in case of emergency—things that were basic to our training, Baranov would tell his interrogators.

And what about Mike in Moscow?

Baranov again says he was honest. They had gone over procedure, but he had not told the Americans anything of consequence at that meeting. Molykov was skeptical, and also he didn't believe what Baranov had said about the instructions he had received. Surely, in order to risk meetings with CIA officers in Moscow, there had to be contingency plans, and surely he must have told Mike something of value when they had met.

No, Baranov replied. That was it.

Molykov, incredulous, at that point called a halt to the interrogation. There would be more time, much more, for questions. He put on his jacket and his oversized military cap—under normal circumstances, a KGB general such as Molykov would not be dressed in uniform but in ordinary civilian clothes—and told Baranov he would now be taken back into Moscow for processing.

Then, with the cameras no longer rolling, he added a chilling footnote to the proceedings, one that, in Baranov's mind, all but confirmed the suspicion that someone had betrayed him. Colonel, Molykov said, "Believe me, we know much more about you than you think we do. I strongly advise you against forcing us to disclose our sources."

This, to Baranov's ears, was an open threat. The KGB did not under any circumstances, not even in a closed court session, want to reveal anything about how it had gotten on to the GRU colonel so quickly. It clearly felt the source who had provided the information was too valuable for even a hint of his existence to come up in court. They wanted Baranov to accept his fate—a certain guilty verdict—meekly.

Three KGB officers escorted him through the airport, weaving their way through all the other passengers at Sheremetyevo. Vyacheslav Baranov, trundled into a waiting car, was headed for a cell at Moscow's infamous Lefortovo prison.

I asked Baranov, in the summer of 1999, what he thought

about during that car ride back into town? How much longer did he think he had to live?

He thought, he said, about his Tanya, and his daughters, and what would become of them. And as for himself, "I didn't really think about it. I was in shock."

CHAPTER 13

LEFORTOVO PRISON

Since its construction in the early 1930s, the basement of Lefortovo has contained blocks of prisons. During the Stalin purges, thousands of people died there. During the Soviet era, many spies also were routinely shot with a bullet to the back of the head—trial, verdict, and sentence occurring with the single pull of a trigger.

Baranov did not know what awaited him as four guards at the prison directed him into a six-foot-by-six-foot cell that afternoon. But soon enough, one of the supreme ironies of his story would become clear. The state that he had decided to betray in 1989 no longer existed. The Soviet Union had fallen apart, and then so too had the Soviet government. Boris Yeltsin succeeded Mikhail Gorbachev at the end of 1991 and soon was the president of an independent, democratic Russia.

And with that new country came a new constitution. Boris

Yeltsin himself had come to despise the Communist Party, even as he rose through its ranks, mainly because of its brutal authoritarianism, and its lack of accountability to anyone. The last years of Yeltsin's reign in Moscow—which I covered from 1996 to 2000—were hardly triumphant. They were dominated by economic crises, his own declining health and severe alcoholism, and all too credible charges of corruption. But the fog of that sorry second term should not diminish the memory of what Boris Yeltsin accomplished in his first term; and the new Russian constitution, which included civil liberties granted ordinary citizens unheard of throughout Russia's history (both Tsarist and Communist), is perhaps his important legacy.

The mere fact that Vyacheslav Baranov is alive today and out of prison is an example of that. He was a traitor to a country that no longer existed, and therefore—to the fury of many of his former colleagues in the KGB and GRU—he was going to get a trial. The trial would be conducted under new evidentiary and sentencing codes that the Yeltsin government had adopted and before a judge determined to enforce them.

Sitting in solitary confinement the night of August 11 Baranov did not know any of this. He knew officers of the KGB were, or would soon be, visiting his wife at home, to tell her that her husband had been arrested for espionage. He tried to imagine how enraged and humiliated his Tanya would be. This thought, more than anything, he would insist years later, was what depressed him as he sat in jail at Lefortovo.

For the first few weeks there Baranov's interrogations continued every day, then after that about three times a week over the next several months. Three different men questioned him, but the lead investigator was a man named Oleg Davydkin. Though only in his early thirties, he already had a reputation as one of the KGB's sharpest minds. His approach in questioning Baranov was not particularly confrontational, but it was very thorough. He tried over and over to get the prisoner to contradict things he had said in the initial interrogation at the airport. He was clearly grasping for more evidence that Baranov had turned over material to the Americans, material that could be shown as damaging "to the motherland."

Baranov knew that as long as they could not demonstrate to a judge that he had passed along damaging secrets, he had a chance of receiving a relatively light sentence. At no time, he would say later, did he seriously consider that he might ultimately get taken to "the wall" and shot, as in Stalinist times. He was determined to fight in court, and he spent most of his time in prison, outside the interrogation sessions with Davydkin, mulling over how to present his case.

The GRU and the KGB kept seeking delays in the trial's start. Often these requests were for bogus reasons. Even though this was the new Russia, not everything had changed. Under these circumstances, the two still-powerful spy agencies got their way. So for more than a year, Baranov sat in Lefortovo, in his dismal six-by-six cell.

The toughest moment of all during that time came early on, when his wife Tatyana visited him for the first time, just two days after he had been moved from solitary. Baranov describes her as an emotional woman, but on this occasion her anger was tightly controlled. She glared at him when they met in a visitor's pen two floors above Baranov's cell. What do you have to say for yourself? she asked him simply.

Baranov says he had been thinking about what to say to her almost from the moment of his arrest. So he tried to explain that he had thought what he was doing would be the best for all of them, that he had had little hope for his country and the system he served. The entire family would benefit, he had thought.

She cut him off, clearly not wanting to hear it. Nor did she want any details, not then anyway. She said she would try to make sure the children didn't learn "too many details" of their father's arrest, and that they would all manage to get through the ordeal. She was trying to be supportive, he would later recall, but he could see how humiliated she felt. He remembers thinking, at this low moment, that maybe a bullet in the head would be better for all concerned.

Baranov did have occasional visits from one close friend during the early days of his imprisonment, and it was through the efforts of Dmitry, a college classmate, that Baranov was able to secure the services of one of Moscow's most noteworthy attorneys.

Tatyana Georgevna Kuznetsova had earned a reputation during the Soviet era as one of the foremost defenders of dissidents and other "political" prisoners arrested under the system, including several spies who were not among those immediately executed.

Being a defense attorney in the Soviet system was the legal

equivalent of being Charlie Brown trying to kick the football: no matter what, the system would prevail, snatching the ball away no matter how hard you tried. Kuznetsova, however, made a reputation for tenacity, and with her fierce insistence that proceedings involving her clients follow the letter of Soviet law—which she knew, it seemed, backwards and forwards. Soviet attorneys facing her were frequently embarrassed when she would show that they did not know the law as well as she did, or as well as a judge did. The result of this was that on occasion she was able to get reduced sentences for some of her clients.

Baranov knew of her, of course. She had defended GRU spy Alexei Filatov, a sensational case that drew much coverage in the Soviet press when he was arrested in 1986. So he instructed his friend Dmitry to make contact with her, and ask if she would consider taking his case. Baranov was pleased when Dmitry reported back that Kuznetsova had agreed at least to a meeting.

In the course of their first meeting, Baranov told the attorney his entire story. Why he had agreed to spy, when it had happened, and how many meetings he had had. He told her also of the fiasco in trying to make contact with the CIA in Moscow, of his exasperation at how he was handled. And he also told her he was convinced he had been betrayed, probably by a mole somewhere in the American intelligence community.

She told Baranov she needed to know what was the most damaging thing he had told the Americans. He said he felt it was the information about the KAL 007 black box. She was skeptical. She asked if he was sure there wasn't anything more, and he said no. Kuznetsova told Baranov she would get in touch with his friend Dmitry in about a week with her decision.

A week later, Dima visited Baranov and gave what amounted to the only bit of good news he had had in this, the bleakest period of his life. Mrs. Kuznetsova would take the case. The Russian Federation trial of Vyacheslav Baranov on espionage charges would finally begin on December 17, 1993, more than a full year after his arrest at Sheremetyevo.

It would last four days.

CHAPTER 14

TRIAL OF A LIFETIME

As a GRU officer, Baranov was tried in the Russian Supreme Court, by a so-called Military Collegium, the Soviet and then Russian equivalent of a trial conducted in the United States under the Uniform Code of Military Justice, our armed forces' own penal code. And in the four days it took in a Russian courtroom to convict him of espionage, Baranov learned more than he expected to about the government's case against him. He learned that his initial instinct, that he had been betrayed, was almost certainly true. To the extent that they were compelled in espionage cases to produce evidence against suspects, the KGB and the GRU tended to do so for reasons beyond just convicting someone (after that, a conviction was a foregone conclusion). In Baranov's case, the prosecutor, a man named Mikhail Kudrin, evidently decided that the trial would be a moment to show off, to demonstrate just how clever the KGB's counterintelligence division really was. They would do this via later press reports on the evidence presented in court. (Reporters were not allowed to attend the trial, even though the KGB had wanted a TV camera in the room, presumably to film Baranov's humiliation for the TV segment that would eventually air. But the judge, a man named Vladimir Alexandrovich Yaskin, would have none of it. He tossed the camera out and the thirty or thirty-five KGB officers who were in the room when the trial began. They had no direct connection to the case, so to Baranov's pleasure, Yaskin tossed them, too.)

But if it intended, in court, to prove its cleverness, the KGB's case, in Baranov's eyes anyway, did the opposite. It all but confirmed what it was trying to hide—that an informant had fingered Baranov as a CIA asset. Baranov had been stunned when he saw that the prosecution had introduced into evidence a picture taken of Mike photographing the Kirovskaya phone booth in which he was supposed to look for Baranov's original signal. This was followed by photographs of Baranov visiting the same phone booth on June 15 to leave the signal.

The prosecutor said in court that the KGB was able to nail Baranov because of crack counterintelligence work, that seeing Mike photograph the phone booth showed them that something important was going to take place there, and that since observing Mike, they had had the booth under twenty-four-hour surveillance (and thus presumably were taking a picture of everyone who entered it for over six months in order to get the shot of Baranov in the booth).

This was obviously bunk. First, the photos were taken from the exact same spot, a window on a high floor in the building across the street, looking down on the booth. This meant that the booth was under surveillance before Mike ever got there to take his photograph. Second, the idea that the booth was under constant surveillance for nearly six months, while the KGB waited for "something" to happen, was preposterous. However meticulous and disciplined the Russian security services may have been relative to their U.S. counterparts, they weren't that meticulous.

There was more. On the second day of the trial, the prosecution revealed that Baranov's apartment had also been under surveillance since spring 1990. Baranov kicked himself when he heard this, because he recalled that his upstairs neighbors had hurriedly, and mysteriously, moved out of the building around that time. At the time, he hadn't given it much thought, but moving from a relatively decent flat in Moscow was by no means a routine thing for most Russian families (at least, not during the Soviet era or early Yeltsin era). It was the KGB who had moved into the flat above him.

The evidence thus showed that KGB counterintelligence was onto Baranov virtually from the moment he arrived back in Moscow. They knew, he believed, that he had been recruited. Even more remarkable was the specificity of information they had: they had known where he would be leaving his signal for Mike, and they knew *when*. This was not crack intelligence work. Someone with very detailed information about his "case" had given him up. Of that Baranov was certain.

There could be no other credible explanation (even though the Russian press would praise the KGB obsequiously when it ran its stories about the trial after the verdict came down). Who it was, under what circumstances, and whether in fact it was the work of just a single mole were questions that would obsess him for the next six years of his life, and which led him ultimately into the *Newsweek* Moscow office in 1998.

Beyond that, the trial did not provide many surprises. Baranov felt lucky to have Mrs. Kuznetsova on his side. She was impressive, as advertised. The gist of the defense she articulated was that Baranov, while guilty of signing on with the CIA, had not passed on any information of consequence. At the time of his arrest, trying to board the flight to Vienna, he was carrying no classified information. The prosecution never introduced any information that he had ever passed any on. Other than the KAL 007 information, Kuznetsova said, Baranov had not told the Americans anything that had not already been published in the book written by GRU defector Viktor Suvorov in 1984 (*Inside Soviet Military Intelligence*): organization schemes, which divisions were responsible for what, that sort of thing. Ever since the publication of Suvorov's book in the West, this sort of information about the GRU had been out and available for anyone who was curious; it hardly constituted the state secrets that the prosecution needed to establish in order to stick Baranov with the harshest sentence possible. Baranov himself effectively served as his own co-counsel, often addressing the judge and responding directly to the evidence that the prosecution produced. And it was his use of the Suvorov book that produced the trial's oddest and most illuminating moments. When the book was published in the early eighties it not surprisingly created quite a stir in Soviet intelligence circles. It was the first detailed and (mostly) accurate account of the GRU's structure and history ever published publicly. While in Dhaka, Baranov says he was given the book by a KGB officer whom he had befriended, a man named Viktor Primachenko.

At his trial Baranov intended to call Primachenko to the stand simply to get him to confirm that he had given him the book in Dhaka. But on the day he was to testify, Primachenko was nowhere to be found. Yaskin, the judge, asked the clerk of the court what was going on. He was told the witness had been properly served with a subpoena and had said he would be in court at the prescribed hour. That a career KGB officer had not shown up to testify in an espionage trial was, to say the least, highly unusual.

Irritated, Yaskin called a recess, then later that day moved on to other witnesses. Baranov and Kuznetsova wondered what had happened and whether Primachenko's absence boded good or ill. They would soon find out.

The next day, Primachenko appeared, apologizing to the judge by saying his wife had suddenly gotten ill the previous day. Baranov stood and asked him whether, while in Dhaka, he had given him the book by Suvorov. He was surprised by the answer.

"Slava," he said to his friend, "you are mistaken. I never gave you that book." Baranov tried to refresh his memory, but again Primachenko demurred, denying he had given him the

Suvorov book. But in so doing, he slipped up. Suvorov had, in fact, written two books about the GRU, the first of which was called *The Glass House,* a reference to the nickname GRU officers had given to the Khodinka headquarters. *The Glass House* had not received any of the notice that Suvorov's subsequent book did, but during his sessions with Davydkin, the lead investigator, Baranov had gotten the two books confused. He referred to *The Glass House* in talking about the book, when he meant to be referring to *Inside Soviet Military Intelligence.*

When Primachenko made the same mistake on the witness stand, Baranov became immediately suspicious. After the witness stood down, Baranov told Kuznetsova what had just happened. His attorney believed she knew exactly what had happened, and was furious. She believed Primachenko's absence the previous day was now entirely understandable. He had probably gone to Lubyanka, KGB headquarters, for a conference with Davydkin and others. The fact was, Kuznetsova told Baranov, the case against him was not as strong as they would like, so they were trying to punch it up a bit by getting Primachenko to deny he had ever given Baranov the book.

In a conference with Yaskin and Davydkin, she immediately told them of her suspicions, and at Baranov's urging threatened that if she felt the sentence ultimately handed down was too harsh, she would bring allegations of "witness tampering" against the prosecution in an appeal proceeding.

Baranov would later say he thought this episode had helped him. Judge Yaskin's willingness to listen to Kuznetsova's

complaints about the alleged witness tampering showed that
he was taking the trial seriously; this was not going to be a
simple KGB walkover, a show trial from the bad old days. The
Soviet Union was dead, and things were changing. The flap
over *The Glass House* also showed the prosecution that Baranov was not rolling over either. Though he knew a guilty verdict was inevitable—he was, after all, guilty—he was
desperately fighting for a reasonable sentence, given that he
insisted he had never turned over any particularly damaging
information to the Americans.

The effort paid off. On the morning of the trial's fourth
day, a Friday, the prosecution rested its case, asking Judge Yaskin
to sentence Baranov to a minimum ten-year prison term.
Yaskin excused himself for just an hour and a half, then returned with a verdict, typed out on one and a half pages. To the
prosecution's fury, the judge agreed with the thrust of Baranov's case. He got off relatively lightly: he was sentenced, under
Article 64 of the Russian Criminal Code ("Betrayal of the
Motherland") to six years of hard labor, including time already
served.

When the judge read the verdict, Baranov was relieved.
He knew it could have been far, far worse. Six years of hard
labor in a Russian prison camp was not going to be a day at
the beach, but the sentence could have been much longer.
This way he would at least see his family again.

He spent the next three months in Lefortovo, moving from
cell to cell. He was bemused when one of his cellmates turned
out to be none other than Ruslan Imranovich Khasbulatov,

one of the leaders of the failed 1991 coup against Mikhail Gorbachev.

On March 3, 1994, Baranov was moved to the Perm 35 correctional camp deep in the Urals to the east, an infamous home to dissidents during the Soviet era. The camp itself is at least an hour and a half drive from the city of Perm, deep in the woods and far from any other humanity (though wolves can be heard howling at night). It consists of two main low-slung buildings that hold twenty-four cells each: four-foot-by-eight-foot rooms containing bunk beds.

The work in the labor camp was hard, a lot of chopping wood, but not as hard as it had been during the Soviet era, when ill-clothed prisoners were often forced to work outside, breaking rocks in subzero temperatures. In 1999 a guard at the camp told me when I visited that Baranov was pretty much a "model prisoner." He did his work, was cordial to the other inmates, and generally spent most of the time by himself, reading and translating books from Russian into English.

But that wasn't all he did. Knowing that he would eventually get out of prison, he obsessed about his case, in the hope that one day he might again get in touch with the Americans and, perhaps, learn who had given him up. He put together a minutely detailed time line of his case. He tried to envision scenarios other than betrayal: could he have been tailed in Dhaka without his knowledge? Were communications somehow compromised at the CIA? (This, ironically, would be a theory briefly favored in Washington while the KGB was rolling up the Ames network—before the CIA was willing to accept the reality that someone at the agency had blood on his hands.) For Baranov this was unknowable, of course. But his "slapdash" handling, as he called it, by the CIA, led him to many dark theories, none of which were flattering for an agency he had come to distrust.

In truth, he never really wavered from the idea that there had to be a mole. Vince, at the meeting where Baranov was christened "Agent Tony," had told him only *ten* people in Washington would know his true identity. So that meant it was highly unlikely that he was blown by some low-level cipher clerk who happened across his name in some poorly coded message. For the next four years, deeply depressed and lonely, Baranov would think to himself thousands of times: there had to be a mole. There had to be a mole.

In Washington, there was, in fact, a very serious mole hunt underway as Baranov endured solitary confinement in Lefortovo. By late 1992, the FBI had had enough of the CIA's stubborn resistance to the idea that there had to be a traitor in its midst. The agency's network of Russian agents had been blown apart, and now the FBI had narrowed a list of suspects to ten. By March of 1993, the list was down to five. On March 15, the head of the FBI's investigation, a senior agent named Tim Caruso, received an eighty-five-page report about the suspects. Of the five, Aldrich Ames was number one. The report's author was Jim Milburn, the FBI's most knowledgeable agent about Russian intelligence. Almost a year later, in February of 1994, the FBI arrested Aldrich Ames not far from his house in Northern Virginia. It was less than a month later that Vyacheslav Baranov was transferred to Perm 35 to serve out the rest of his prison term.

CHAPTER 15

THE GULAG

The years in Perm 35 took their toll on Baranov. His teeth deteriorated badly; he lost weight. The stress and the agonizing, and a diet that consisted mainly of bread and soup, would eventually lead to a serious stomach ailment that, by the time we were dealing with each other and with the FBI and CIA, would become life threatening.

In September of 1995, after more than a year at the Camp, Baranov gave an ill-advised interview to a sensational *60 Minutes*-like television show called *Top Secret,* which did a long segment on his case, one of several that were produced glorifying the brilliance of the post-Soviet KGB.

In it Baranov appears in his dark blue prison garb and a blue cap. He has a wispy mustache, and looks drawn and defeated. Yet in the interview he tries to explain himself, sucking on a cigarette, speaking thoughtfully about his case. It was a moment when his basic self-confidence—the self-awareness that he was an intelligent man who throughout his life had (in his mind, anyway) made sane, thoughtful decisions—betrayed him. In the piece, his musings look silly, portrayed as they were against the supposedly heroic exploits of the intelligence services to protect the motherland from this devious traitor. Did he really think he was going to get a fair shake on Russian national television? Later, typically, he said his decision to grant the interview was done simply out of a deep desire to break the tedium of life in the camp.

"What did I care how they were going to portray me? I could explain myself, and they could do with it whatever they wanted."

His physical decline was not surprising. The tedium and hardship of life in the Gulag broke only occasionally. His Tanya, for all her private rage at what he had done, never abandoned him, for which he was deeply grateful. Prisoners at Perm 35 were allowed visitors every few months, and Tatyana made the nine-hour train journey from Moscow routinely. They would chat about their daughters, of course, but Baranov would also ask about political developments in Yeltsin's Russia. How were things going? Was the government stable? Was there a chance for another coup attempt? Baranov was intensely interested because any rollback would almost surely mean bad news for him.

But Tatyana was at best apolitical, and at worst someone who tended to blame the nation's current privations (which were enormous) on the new government, rather than on sixty years of Communist rule (and in this, of course, she was like millions of her fellow citizens). Baranov would learn more from the occasional visits he got from Kuznetsova, his attorney, who also visited occasionally. The two had become friends in the run-up to his trial, and he appreciated greatly her willingness to come all the way from Moscow to see him.

Still, these were rare respites. Perm 35 when Baranov was there may not quite have been the Gulag of the Stalin era (captured most horrifyingly in the classic Eugenia Ginzburg memoir *Journey into the Whirlwind*), but prison is prison. The two bunk beds in each cell are made of steel rods; there is a pit toilet in the corner of each cell. There is no privacy. The heating during the long Urals winter was only just adequate.

If under such circumstances anything can be described as a blessing, for Baranov there were two: One was that the guards did not treat him with any particular cruelty. He was, after all, guilty of what he had been charged with, betraying his country by spying for the United States. But prison guard Anatoly Krasyanov later spoke of Baranov as only another prisoner, one who was treated neither better nor worse than anyone else. Baranov affirms that that was indeed the case.

The second thing for which Baranov would turn out to be grateful occurred toward the end of his incarceration. It is the event that set in motion the bizarre sequence of events that got me into the middle of Baranov's life. This was the date when my colleague Andy Nagorski traveled to the camp with a group of former prisoners, all of them prominent dissidents. That he was able to do this, go to what remained an active prison camp in Russia with a group of dissidents who had been imprisoned there, should remind us again of how much had changed since Boris Yeltsin had come to power.

Nagorski would do a story that appeared in *Newsweek* a few weeks later on the recollections of these men as they strolled about their former prison: what "offenses" they were there for, what their existence was like, how they were treated. To say the least, visits like this were unusual, and not surprisingly, word quickly got around the camp that a bunch of Soviet-era dissidents were wandering around with a correspondent from *Newsweek*. Baranov learned of it from one of the guards.

It was this visit that put the idea in his mind that perhaps someday, if necessary, he could try to get in touch with the *Newsweek* bureau chief as a way to reach the U.S. government. That he was thinking this at the time, as he insists he was, shows just how obsessed he was with his mole theory. Not only did he believe the U.S. government still owed him the "full faith and protection" of which Vince had assured him in Dhaka, but there was a spy in their midst, and he felt his case made that clear.

In April of 1997, Baranov learned in a very personal way that some things had changed in Russia under Boris Yeltsin. The fact that he caused no one any trouble while in prison— more than a year in solitary at Lefortovo starting in the late summer of 1992 and more than three years at Perm 35—made him eligible for parole. Remarkably, the former full colonel of the GRU who had turned CIA spy was granted it. On April

22, Lenin's birthday, he walked out of the camp, where Tatyana greeted him. They embraced briefly, and then got in a car she had hired for the long ride back to the Perm train station, and the trip back to Moscow.

On the terms of the parole, the government kept his passport. He could not travel anywhere outside of Russia that required a visa. Other than that, he was "a free man."

A free man, but a pariah, even if it was the new Russia. Baranov would have to find a job, some means to help support himself and his family. That meant he would have to find someone, somewhere, who was willing to hire a traitor.

That, as far as he was concerned, was a stopgap only, a temporary measure to make ends meet until he could carry out his real business. He would do whatever it took to get back in touch with those who had embraced him in Dhaka. He would find out what happened. He would tell them of the spy in their midst. And he would get the agency to make good: to relocate him and his family to the United States, with a big chunk of money stashed in a bank account waiting for them. This is what would consume him from that point forward. He just didn't know how extraordinarily difficult all that was going to be.

CHAPTER 16

IN THE COLD

Aldrich Ames's deadly nine-year run of betrayal ended in February of 1994, when he was arrested by the FBI. His attorney, Plato Cacheris, quickly convinced him to cut a deal with the government, and he did, agreeing to recount in detail all the information he had turned over to Moscow, in return for his life. After the Ames debriefing, it became clear to the FBI mole hunters, Jim Milburn included, that there remained unexplained cases in which CIA assets had disappeared or been arrested. Baranov's was one of them (but not the only one). This meant that the elation FBI director Louis Freeh felt at the time of the Ames arrest didn't last long. By early 1994—as Baranov sat in the labor camp in Perm—another mole-hunting team had been put together and was beginning its work.

The CIA, having just come through the trauma and the extraordinary embarrassment of the Ames affair, was not exactly thrilled with this. Publicly, the agency had taken a vicious, if deserved, pounding in Congress and in the press. Typical was an editorial cartoon that had two FBI agents burst into an office with a sign on the door reading "CIA Headquarters." There sitting at a desk is a mole; that is, the four-legged kind. The mole is wearing a Russian hat. He has a suitcase next to his desk with one of those bumper stickers on it that says, "I Love Moscow." The agents are saying to the mole: "Okay, Ames, you can't fool us anymore, you're under arrest!"

The idea that there might be yet another penetration in the agency—which, as the investigation slowly progressed over the next two years, is what the FBI team was coming to believe—was not welcome news in Langley. As one of the investigators said later, "The [agency] either wanted to pin every one of their losses on Ames, or they didn't want to hear about it."

When Baranov got out on parole in April of 1997, there were things he needed to do before he could begin to pursue his obsession, getting in touch with the CIA and trying to find out who had betrayed him. He needed to find a job. For someone in his situation, a newly released prisoner who had done prison time for treason, that wasn't going to be easy. He had several friends who had left the military (there was no way he was going to approach any former GRU acquaintances) and were now trying to make a go of it as businessmen in Russia's newly free (if chaotic and corrupt) economy. Baranov found it hard even to approach his old friends, knowing what an awkward position it would put them in. Nonetheless, he needed some income to help support his family, as well as to help stay sane. All either never got back to him, or just made up excuses as to why they could not hire him.

In August of 1997, four months after getting out of Perm 35, Baranov briefly gave up the job search and made his first effort at getting back in touch with the U.S. government. He did not want to risk showing up at the U.S. embassy. He was, after all, out on parole and that would obviously land him right back at Perm 35. He could however freely travel to Ukraine, the former Soviet republic west of Russia, without any travel documents. He had a good friend in Kiev and decided he would pay him a visit, and at the same time scope out the U.S. Embassy there. If it was not under heavy surveillance from the KGB (called the SBU in the newly independent Ukraine), he might just risk trying to get a meeting with the FBI's legal attaché there.

The train trip to Kiev was uneventful. Baranov was not followed, and did not appear to be picked up by any surveillance once he got there. He went to his friend Dmitry's apartment, spent the night, and then went to the embassy the next morning. He strolled around the block casually, and what he saw disappointed him. The building was under surveillance from what he identified as at least four plainclothes security officers. (This was in addition to the uniformed security guards outside the embassy.) The plainclothesmen were not making much of an effort to be inconspicuous. They were simply hanging out at spots across the street from the embassy, not pretending to be doing anything other than watching who was going in and coming out.

He did the same thing the next day, just to make sure that that level of surveillance was routine. To his disappointment, it was. But Baranov had another option for trying to reach the FBI in a way that did not involve the embassy in Russia or Ukraine. He had a friend, like Dmitry a Ukrainian, who had emigrated to Canada a few years earlier. Baranov gave a letter to Dmitry to post from Kiev. In it, he asked his friend in Canada—another former air force officer—to find out the name of the FBI representative in the U.S. Embassy in Ottawa, and to send a letter back to Dima in Kiev with the name. (Baranov had not wanted to risk sending a letter on his own from either Moscow or Kiev lest it be intercepted and read.)

Several weeks passed, and the name came back. The FBI legat (legal advisor) in Ottawa was Jerry Rose. Baranov wrote two letters to Rose, sent again from Dima, to his friend in Canada, and then on to the U.S. Embassy. The letters explained briefly who he was, and that he thought *someone* from the U.S. government would be interested in hearing from him. Several more weeks passed, with no response to either letter. In December, Baranov again traveled to Ukraine, and from his friend's apartment sent a fax to Rose at his office in Ottawa. Again, no response. Irritated, and afraid this was going to be his best shot at getting the attention of someone in the FBI, he took a major risk. He phoned the embassy in Ottawa and managed to get Rose on the phone. The FBI agent said he didn't have time to talk, and hung up. A few days later, Baranov tried to call again. This time Rose was rude, told Baranov not to call back, and hung up.

Baranov was furious. Rose clearly had not taken him, or what his letters said, seriously. How could he conclude otherwise? If Rose had made the least bit of an effort to verify that Baranov was who he said he was, why wouldn't he deal with him? Surely, sitting in Ottawa, he wasn't exactly inundated with phone calls from former GRU colonels who said they had signed on with the agency and then spent years in prison for their efforts? (Rose, when I contacted him in 2001, refused to discuss this incident.)

The episode, not surprisingly, only added to the bitterness Baranov already harbored for those he had dealt with in the U.S. government. It is, ultimately, what led him to my office, and to reveal so much of his story to a journalist, in the somewhat desperate hope that I would believe him, and bring his case to the attention of the embassy in Moscow. (He was still unwilling to take the risk of just showing up at the embassy gate and hoping for the best.)

Though he was out of Perm, and obviously grateful for that, Baranov was a frustrated, angry man at the end of 1997. The only thing that had gone right since getting out of the camp was that another old friend actually had managed to get him a job. The head of Russia's kickboxing federation, which sponsors tournaments and in general tries to promote the sport of kickboxing, agreed to take him on as an assistant. It was, frankly, a humiliating position—paying only about $50 a month—but Baranov's position within Russia was itself humiliating. But he needed the money, and he needed something to occasionally take his mind off his conundrum. His plight was, however bizarrely, soon going to be in my hands. And he didn't know me, and I didn't know him, from Adam. Obviously, neither of us at that point could have imagined where events would soon take us.

He would eventually get his hearing though, for two reasons. The first was his own persistence. And the second was the fact that in Washington, where rumors of another mole—that is, a post–Aldrich Ames mole—had long circulated, some powerful people were coming to the same conclusion that Baranov had reached. He had been betrayed, and he could not have been betrayed by Ames. There *was* another mole. All Baranov wanted was an opportunity to help the U.S. government find him.

CHAPTER 17

CROSSING THE LINE

It was his anger, frustration, and desperation that had led him to my office in 1998. After several meetings I had, as I've said, come to believe at least the gist of his story. But coming to believe it and then acting on it, in the way he wanted me to—going to the embassy on his behalf—was not something I was yet ready to do. I had lots of other stuff to do, and I was also still trying to sort out the implications of all this. I was interested in him as a story, but should I act as his intermediary with the U.S. government? I certainly never imagined back then that I would end up as deep in his story as I did, and I wasn't moving on this as quickly as he desired, because *something* about it was still making me vaguely queasy.

So after our initial meetings in the summer and then early autumn of 1998, I put Baranov off, using any excuse I could. I was busy; I was out of town on assignment; I couldn't get hold of anyone at the embassy who would deal with me. But he kept showing up in the office, and since I remained intrigued, and, frankly, often enjoyed talking to him about other things, such as what was going on in his country, our meetings, in the early part of 1999, became more frequent. As our relationship evolved from one of wariness to what became friendship, we both let our guard down. One evening, over beers across the street from the *Newsweek* bureau at the John Bull Pub, he started naming names. That is to say, he started naming and describing the people who had recruited him and then handled him at the agency. Brad. Vince. Mike. The volleyball game in Dhaka. The meeting at the train station back in Moscow. It was as if he were making a final plea: C'mon, I'm telling you *everything;* you *have* to do something.

He was also, to my mind, making a pretty good case that there had to be another mole. When Baranov came out of prison, he learned about the Ames case, and wanted of course to know whether it was possible that Ames was his man. But the information he had about the case was thin and came mostly from Russian press reports, which were sketchy at best. I gave him a copy of a well-reported book about the case, *Nightmover* by David Wise, and it had an electrifying effect on Baranov.[*]

---

[*] *Nightmover* is the best book on Ames from the CIA side, in part because Wise was the only journalist Ames agreed to talk to, and however loathsome a character Ames may be, the book benefits from that. The best book from the FBI's side of the story—picking up with the "Playactor" investigation and then through to the arrest of *Nightmover* himself (the code name the bureau gave Ames)—is Peter Maas's *Killer Spy.*

There was a single fact that had jumped out at him, and made it clear in his mind—and indeed, he had to think, in the mind of anyone who was even remotely paying attention—there could be no way Ames gave him up to Moscow. As he put it later, in his vernacular English, "It hit me like a ton of bricks." What had become clear is that the time lines of the two men—Ames and Baranov, and what happened to them—precluded Ames in his case.

When Ames was in Washington, as head of the counterintelligence branch in the Soviet–East European division at the agency, he indeed knew the names and positions of virtually every Soviet agent the CIA employed, in the former Soviet Union and elsewhere. But when he was in Rome, as deputy station chief, he did not have, and could not get, that kind of information. And Aldrich Ames was in Rome when Vyacheslav Baranov was recruited, or as he puts it, when he "walked in." He reread the relevant sections of the book a second and third time, to make sure he wasn't missing something. He wasn't. Surely, he felt, there *had* to be an ongoing investigation in Washington, because there *had* to be another mole. And if that was true, he said to me over and over, wouldn't the FBI want to talk to him? And wouldn't the CIA want to hear from him?

For me to do what he wanted—to go to someone at the embassy and say, look, this guy has pitched up on my doorstep, and this is what he says, and therefore as far as I can tell, the CIA owes him big time—was crossing a threshold. At some level I knew that, even though I never said it to him straight out. American journalists weren't supposed to get in the middle of spy games. The Church Committee hearings of the mid-1970s had put an end to that, and basically for very good reasons.

The first reason was that, for a foreign correspondent, suspicion that you were aiding and abetting the CIA was always a pretext for a host government to throw you out, ending your assignment. That never pleases the bosses at headquarters. Beyond that, if a government has a shred of evidence that a journalist actually *is* cooperating with the CIA, it's enough to get you arrested or, in some places, even killed. That was certainly true during the Cold War and was true even after that in enduring hot spots like the Middle East, Africa, and, yes, the former Soviet Union. And if, in fact, it *was* true that you were involved in espionage, and you still weren't arrested or killed, basically you were finished as a journalist anyway because your credibility, the only currency you have, as the cliché has it, would be shot.

But the reality was also that I wanted to write this guy's story, and in order for the story to go anywhere, in order for me to find out whether in fact Vyacheslav Baranov was real or whether he was Memorex, I needed to cross the line, at least a little bit. I needed to go to someone at the embassy and let him or her know what was going on.

Two things, in my own mind, finally overrode the concerns I had. First, I wrote a long memo to my editors in New York, saying I was on to what was potentially a good story, but one that hadn't played out yet. To see where it was going, I had to go to the government, even though this potentially was going to complicate matters for me.

They responded positively, arguing that as long as I was upfront with everybody (as I had been), that I was pursuing this as a story, there wasn't a problem.

The other thing I thought, simply, was that this guy had been screwed. Whether or not I believed his assertion that there was another mole somewhere in the U.S. security apparatus—and the fact was I had heard only his side of the story and, as persuasive as it was, I was hardly in a position to draw any conclusions—he had plainly been badly mishandled by the agency when he was working for them as a very valuable agent; and his treatment once getting out of the Gulag, to be totally ignored, was, to me, infuriating and inexcusable. All I could think of was what the agency must be like in the post–Aldrich Ames environment, and that someone like Baranov, if he was telling the truth, simply represented another problem they had no stomach for dealing with. (I didn't know this to be true, but having read the Ames books at this point, that was all I could conclude.)

Baranov deserved at least a hearing, I thought, and I was in a position at least to get someone's attention in the government, to see if we could arrange that hearing. I would later half jokingly tell my wife that it was time to stop worrying about the potential journalistic conflicts of interest, or the possibility that I would be tossed in jail or out of the country, and start acting like a human being. (She was not amused. From the beginning she never thought I should have anything to do with this guy, because she thought it was going to end up as trouble. We agreed to disagree.)

So one morning late in 1998, I called my friend Mike Hurley at the U.S. Embassy in Moscow. Mike was the public affairs officer, the first contact for the press (both Russian and foreign), which means, in the tumultuous Yeltsin era, he was pretty busy. The United States had of course bought into Yeltsin heavily—in 1991, who wouldn't have?—but that meant that for practically every issue that came up, particularly during Yeltsin's second term—the United States had something to answer for: corruption (were we looking the other way?); the looming economic crisis and subsequent default; "loose nukes," the idea that terrorists had been able to steal either warheads or highly enriched uranium from Russian nuclear sites (which we were paying to help safeguard); the bloody conflict in Chechnya (which President Bill Clinton, in order to defend Yeltsin, once compared to our Civil War); the never-ending murkiness about the true state of Yeltsin's health (C'mon, *someone* in the U.S. government must know the truth about how bad it is! Tell us!). The list went on.

Hurley, soft-spoken and mostly accommodating (at least to establishment press types like the *Newsweek* bureau chief), was pretty easy to deal with. So when I called him and said we needed to talk about something I couldn't really discuss on the phone, he agreed and we met the next day in the cafeteria on the ground floor of the embassy, just about five minutes from my office.

I brought with me the thick dossier Baranov had compiled—the time line, the details of his case, with all the names of his case officers and all the screwups, plus his brief for the prosecution, which held that there was another, post–Aldrich Ames mole somewhere in the U.S. government. I told Mike that I wanted to do a story on this guy, but that I obviously needed to verify his bona fides. I remember trying to make it seem as if I wasn't sure whether I believed him or not, but I'm not sure how good a job I did.

Hurley responded as I had felt he would. As a press officer, he's hardly going to promise anything after getting hit with something like that out of the blue. So he just said that yes, guys like this come over the transom all the time. They usually just wanted money; and half the time, he said, they were crazy.

I had to laugh. I told him, yeah, the first time Baranov had shown up it was after a whole slew of benighted souls had come to my office seeking favors; I had begun to think I was auditioning candidates for a Russian game show: who's the nuttiest of them all? But then I did say that I had concluded that Baranov was probably not a nut, and that I would be interested in whatever response he might be able to glean from people in a position to know. He said he would run it by the "appropriate people" and see what they said.

I was skeptical. Hurley's initial response was what I had thought it would be—Oh yeah, right, another "spy" coming in from the cold who wants to relocate to the United States and live happily ever after. I also thought that since Baranov had been so obviously stiff-armed since his release from Perm 35, nothing would change. Even if Mike did run it by the CIA and FBI folks in the embassy, they'd want nothing to do with it, *particularly* since a reporter was in the middle of it. And it was funny. Because at some level, I thought, having done my journalistic duty, as well as my duty as a human being, that was going to be the end of it. I'd get kissed off, just as Baranov had been, and that would be that.

I was wrong. Two days later, Hurley called me at the bureau. Could I come over? The FBI's legal attaché in the embassy, a guy named Bill Kinane, wanted to meet with me to discuss the matter we had talked about over lunch. Fine, I said, when?

"How about now?"

"Now?"

"Yes."

I said, give me an hour and I'll be there. I was, I admit, taken aback by the speed of the response. Baranov and I had a policy that he would get in touch with me when he felt he wanted to meet, but now I wondered whether I should get in touch with him to tell him what had happened. I decided not to, if only because I would have more information for him after the meeting with Kinane, and that pretty much anything Kinane wanted to know in a first meeting I would be able to answer.

So I went over. I had dealt once before with Kinane—who was the first FBI legat ever in the U.S. Embassy post–Cold War and was now serving a second term—on a small corruption story I had done. He was an FBI agent who was, on one level, straight out of central casting—a big Irishman from Brooklyn who reminded me of my grandfather, an ex–New York City cop, a likable, regular guy, with whom it would become easy to spend time at the embassy's Liberty Bar talking NFL football. (Having been based for much of his domestic career with the FBI in San Francisco, Kinane had become a 49ers fan.) But the central casting image was somewhat misleading, because he spoke fluent Russian, and in an era when Russian organized-crime groups were rapidly expanding in the United States and elsewhere, that made him a relatively elite officer within the bureau.

We met in the cafeteria, and over coffee exchanged pleasantries, and then he got down to business. He had taken the material I had given to Mike Hurley, Baranov's notes and time line, and sent it to Washington. And Washington had responded. "They"—no mention at this point as to who "they" were—were interested. Clearly curious about the whole case and how it had ended up on my doorstep, Kinane asked a series of questions as to how I had gotten to know Baranov. How often did I meet with him? Where did I meet with him? Was there any evidence that we were under surveillance? How the hell would I know, I responded. He said, does *he* think he is under surveillance? I said I thought not.

He said he was going to send another fax to Washington based on our conversation, and await further instructions. But he was going to need to meet with me again. He then said should I need to get in touch with him, I should simply call him or his secretary and say I wanted to meet for a cup of coffee. I was under no circumstances to mention Baranov's name on the phone. If he called me, he would do the same. "Let's have a cup of coffee."

This had not been the response I was expecting. Kinane, as easygoing as he was naturally, was clearly uncomfortable with this whole situation, in part because he was basically just playing messenger between me and the counterintelligence people in Washington. But his body language, his inability in that first meeting to make real eye contact, made *me* uncomfortable.

Something was up here. Clearly. Baranov was real. I didn't know where this was going, but it was going somewhere. I reminded Kinane I was pursuing this as a journalist. He nodded. I said that even though it was our practice for Baranov to get in touch with me, I was going to try to call him in order to tell him Washington was, in fact, interested in his case. After his years of suffering, I was sure this alone would electrify him. This was contact, something that he had not had since getting out of prison. It was the reason he had walked into my office in the first place.

Kinane looked uncomfortable, but he didn't object. Just remember, he said, "Call and say you want to have a cup of coffee if you need to meet. I'll do the same. We'll be in touch."

It was bitterly cold and sunny that day. Outside the embassy, at the entrance to the public areas like the gym and the cafeteria where American citizens like me could get in with a special pass, my driver Yuri awaited in *Newsweek's* battered old blue Volvo. On that bright, freezing afternoon, I violated, I suppose, spy rule number one: I immediately did something out of the ordinary. Wanting to clear my head, I told Yuri to go back to the bureau without me. I walked, going past the Russian White House, which sits next to the embassy, and then took a right across the bridge and up Kutuzovsky Prospekt. Not a long walk, but one I needed. This was going to be a story after all. Baranov, as I knew, was not a nut.

I got back to the office in about twenty minutes. For the first time, I called Baranov on his mobile phone. He seemed taken aback when he heard my voice, but I simply said, why don't we meet for a cup of coffee.

He said fine, where and when. I didn't want this meeting, or frankly any more of our meetings, to occur in my office. I said let's get together at the Starlight Diner, which was the ultimate ex-pat hangout in Moscow. He knew just from the fact that I had called him that something was up. He asked when to be there, and so that evening, we met at six o'clock, just two more customers, sitting amidst the American businessmen and journalists and the Russian yuppies, ogling the cute miniskirted waitresses, and eating overpriced hamburgers.

I told him exactly what had happened. I told him his dossier was on someone's desk in Washington. I said I hadn't been told whose, but it was someone who was interested.

He took this all in with less evident emotion than I had anticipated. He asked when I thought I would see Kinane next.

I said I didn't know, but I would alert him when the next meeting was coming.

He just thanked me, and said something to the effect that maybe, finally, he was getting somewhere. He was right. The spy games had well and truly begun.

CHAPTER 18

GREECE IS NICE THIS TIME OF YEAR

It was about a week later when, at Baranov's request, I phoned Kinane again and asked if we could have "a cup of coffee." We set a meeting for later that day at the embassy, this time at the Liberty Bar, one floor up from the embassy's basketball court and workout room. It was a dark place that served decent German beer and popcorn, and showed American sports events on an overhead TV. It was particularly popular with the so-called TDY crowd, the people sent to Moscow on temporary tours of duty, most of whom during my time there were construction workers building a new embassy going up right next to the old one. (This in itself was an expensive legacy of the spying game: the previous "new" embassy had been discovered to be so riddled with Soviet wiretaps that the government had to tear it down and start over.) I told him Baranov wanted to know whether there had been any further communication from Washington. Having waited this long for any contact at all, he was understandably anxious to see things move ahead.

It wasn't going to be that easy. Kinane squirmed a bit, but then laid out the difficulty as his (as yet unidentified) contacts in Washington saw it: the FBI was indeed interested in what Baranov had to say, as he had said in our previous meeting. But neither the bureau nor the CIA was willing to risk a meeting, as Kinane put it, "anywhere in the former Soviet Union." The feeling was, he said, that it might put Baranov in jeopardy again. After he had already served time for espionage, forcing him to meet with U.S. agents again in "hostile" territory would put him at too much risk.

I offered that I thought he was more than willing to take that risk, given how long such a meeting had been in coming, as long as the proper precautions were taken. Kinane waved me off. "Not going to happen," he said, "it's already been decided."

At the time I didn't know how to evaluate this extreme aversion to risk. Given that I at this point was acting as Baranov's intermediary and, in some sense, advocate, I suspected it might be more of the same: a stalling tactic, an excuse to continue *not* dealing with him. I still didn't think much of the possibility that there was a real live mole in play here. These events had happened a while ago, and I naïvely assumed that even if Baranov was right about someone other than Aldrich Ames betraying him, whoever that was was probably long gone.

(Baranov himself conceded that that was possible, but for obvious reasons was far more determined to force the issue, to try to get a sense, as he would put it over and over, "of what exactly happened.") Therefore the idea that the Russians might arrest him again seemed overly cautious to me.

But as Kinane said, the decision had been made, and this obviously presented real difficulties for all of us involved. Kinane brought them up. The U.S. government wanted to find a way to move me out of the middle of all this, for obvious reasons. I said I appreciated that and certainly wanted that to happen. But, he went on, it wasn't clear to them how to make that happen quickly.

A big part of the problem was the terms of Baranov's parole from the Gulag. He had gotten out early, but the government retained his passport. He was not allowed to travel outside of Russia and those former Soviet republics which did not require a visa for Russian citizens to enter. Thus, given that the FBI and CIA had foreclosed a meeting "anywhere in the former Soviet Union," we were stuck. Baranov couldn't get *out* of the former Soviet Union, and they wouldn't try to get in. And that, Kinane didn't need to say, left me in the middle. He said Washington was trying to figure out a way to get a meeting arranged with Baranov, but until then there would probably be no news. He again asked that I check back with him in a week or so.

* * *

Baranov seemed irritated at this news, but not as angry as I had expected. He said he thought the agency was being overly cautious, but he hoped he could believe Kinane's assertion that they were working out a game plan. Looking back on this, I think Baranov felt at this point that since much of what he had to say—the details of his argument about another mole—was in the hands of people who worked on such things, that he could no longer be ignored. I had adopted his previous cynicism, while now he seemed quietly hopeful, calmer than he had been.

Another week passed, and I got a better idea as to why he had begun to have some hope.

Kinane and I met again in the Liberty Bar. We ordered beers and engaged in a little small talk. We briefly discussed what was happening in Russia, and I tried without success to pry to see if he had any information or gossip about the various corruption scandals that swirled about the Yeltsin Kremlin. Once it was clear to Kinane that no one around us could hear what we were saying, he got down to business.

"Do you have any plans," he asked, "to be in the States anytime soon?"

No, I said, I hadn't.

What about western Europe, he asked? Any travel plans, either for work or pleasure?

Well, yes, in fact. Within the next couple of weeks I was going to head to Athens on a Russian money-laundering story. After that, I said, I planned to take a long weekend on the island of Crete, a beautiful spot in the Mediterranean. Why?

Kinane said that his colleagues in Washington, unable to meet with Baranov for the time being, wanted to meet with me. In effect, they wanted to debrief me, question me about all of our meetings and the information Baranov had provided in the dossier that Kinane had sent on to FBI headquarters in Washington. Would I agree to such a meeting?

I said, again, that as long as everyone involved understood that at some point I was going to write about all this, yes, I would agree.

He said he'd get back to me.

I relayed this news to Baranov and he was obviously pleased, and for good reason. He drew the only sensible conclusion. It was a sign of their seriousness. He was, finally, back on the radar of the people who had, as far as he could tell, thoroughly abandoned him. Finally there was movement, even if it did not yet involve direct contact with him.

Two days later Kinane called and, using the coffee code, asked that I come over. I did. He wanted to know the specific dates of my trip to Greece, and where I would be staying, both in Athens and then later in Crete. It was the nature of these meetings that basically each question he posed would take another day for me to answer. I needed to go back to the office and check the specific dates and the phone numbers of the hotels I had booked. Then it would take another day for him to relay my reply to Washington and get its response. Never would Kinane ask me a substantive question on the phone. I could tell it pained him even to be on the phone for ten seconds with me, aware that our phones in the bureau were tapped.

The following day I provided the dates and the names and phone numbers of the hotels I had booked, and we fixed a meeting for the next day.

So around five on a late winter day in 1999, I arrived at the embassy, curious about what Kinane would have to say.

He made me wait for about ten minutes in the Liberty Bar, and I nervously gulped one small beer waiting for him. He arrived finally and I think was pleased to see that the place was empty, except for us and the bartender.

Okay, he said, it was set. There would be a meeting. Two agents from the FBI would meet me not in Athens but in Crete. They would arrive in the lobby of my hotel about noon. Be in your room, he said. One of the agents would call and identify himself as "a friend of Bill's."

"The guy's name," Kinane added, "is Jim Milburn."

If there was a single moment, as this story unfolded, when the gravity of what exactly was happening became clear to me, in a way that was simply stunning, this was it. I don't know if I had been in denial in some way, or whether my own naïveté had prevented me from seeing this affair as anything more than basically an interesting story, and one that maybe really wasn't going anywhere. Beyond that, I simply hoped somehow things would be set right for Baranov. But never in a million years did I expect to find myself in the middle of the highest-profile manhunt since the one that finally got Aldrich Ames.

I had read all of the books written about Ames—*Nightmover*, the one I had given Baranov, as well as several others. So I knew who Jim Milburn was. He was one of the two FBI counterintelligence agents who had teamed up with a handful of agency investigators, and together they had finally nailed Ames. Milburn was the one who had, late in the game, written the eighty-five-page report that had put Ames at the top of a list of five suspects.

In the Liberty Bar at that moment, my head was swimming. I tried not to let on how stunned I was. I'm not sure I succeeded. I said something like, "Milburn? He was involved with the Ames stuff, wasn't he?"

Kinane nodded.

"Milburn is coming to meet *me* in Greece?"

"Yes."

I said nothing. I was vaguely in shock. I can tell you what I was thinking, though. I was thinking: Holy shit.

Kinane left. I had another beer and tried to get a grip. I had to get in touch with Baranov right away. I raced back to the bureau and called him. I tried at once to sound casual but to convey the urgency of the need to meet. He said he was busy at the moment, could it wait until tomorrow?

Umm, no, I said.

Okay, he replied. Where?

I said the place we had met last—"Delta," as we had begun referring to the Starlight Diner (the spying stuff becomes insidious).

He got there about an hour later. I told him what had happened at my meeting at the embassy with Kinane. I reminded him who Milburn was, what his role had been in the Ames investigation. If he needed a signal that Washington was taking him and the information he provided seriously, he had gotten it. Big time.

"They are," I said, "presumably not sending one of the guys who got Ames on some wild-goose chase to Greece. I'm sure he hasn't been demoted since then. This is very serious."

Baranov said he understood and smiled thinly. He was obviously pleased, but again there was no real elation. He was closer to where he wanted to be, in direct contact with his former paymasters at the U.S. government, but still had a ways to go. He was getting there, though. He was getting there. He finished his drink and said we would have to meet again before I left.

Right, I said.

He left the diner. I paid the bill, gazed at the waitresses, and thought, *What* in God's name have I gotten myself into?

CHAPTER 19

ELOUNDA BAY

Elounda Bay curls in from the Mediterranean Sea on the northeast side of the island of Crete, and when the sun shines on it, as it does most of the time, the surface of its warm water glistens so intensely blue that it almost hurts to look at it. For decades, wealthy Europeans have spent holidays in the Greek Islands, and Elounda Bay has become one of the premier stops for the private plane and yachting crowd. A few hilly kilometers from a touristy fishing village sit a number of luxurious hotels and resorts, the splashiest of which is called the Elounda Bay Hotel and villas.

I am not a rich European and definitely do not own a yacht. Nonetheless, in the spring of 1999, after a less than edifying reporting trip to Athens on a Russian corruption story I was pursuing, I pitched up in Elounda Bay for a long weekend—a respite from a fairly intense period of work in Moscow that at the time I dearly needed. My Japanese wife and young son were in Tokyo visiting her parents, so I planned just to crash on the beach and recuperate.

I rented a small waterfront villa for a few days with a deck overlooking the bay. A small winding staircase from the villa led down to the warm water below.

Every morning I would get up early and go out for a long swim, and when I'd return, a breakfast of fresh fruit, orange juice, and coffee would be laid out on the table on the deck. I decided being a rich European wasn't a bad deal (if only I could figure out how to become one).

But this trip was obviously not going to be as stress-free as I had hoped. It had been nearly two years since Baranov had walked into my office that afternoon in Moscow, and in this sun-dappled sliver of the Mediterranean, two people were going to show up to prove that his case now had the attention of some very serious people in Washington. The only problem was that I was still in the middle, the intermediary/messenger boy/journalist. And they were two of the U.S. government's chief mole hunters.

At precisely noon, as Kinane had said it would, the phone in my room rang. Jim, "a friend of Bill's," said he was waiting for me in the lobby of the hotel.

I said I'd be right there, and walked up from the villa, wearing a purple tee shirt, orange shorts, and flip-flops. Waiting for me were two casually dressed Americans. Jim Milburn, trim, with reddish hair and looking to be around my age (fortyish) wore a white polo shirt and khakis. He was, as Peter Maas wrote in his book about Aldrich Ames (*Killer Spy*) "renowned within the FBI for his intimate knowledge of Soviet intelligence." His partner, a younger, athletic-looking blond woman, was Lauren Gruendel, a former Drug Enforcement Agency agent who had moved over to the FBI's counterintelligence division a couple of years earlier.

We shook hands, and Milburn asked if there was someplace private we could talk. I said the best place was my room, where we could sit out on the deck, have lunch, and talk without risk of being overheard. Along the way I told him I had been in Athens on a Russian money-laundering story, only to come down here and find an awful lot of Russian money launderers lounging on the beach. Among the rich Europeans vacationing in Crete in the late 1990s were the so-called new Russians, an elite criminal class of well-connected asset strippers, thieves, and money launderers who had gotten famously, obscenely wealthy during the economic chaos of the Yeltsin years.

I led them to my room and invited them to sit at the table on the deck. I went in and ordered salmon sandwiches and a bunch of Diet Cokes from room service. On my way back out, I grabbed all the material I had gathered from Baranov, as well as notes I had made about my many meetings with him. I didn't know exactly what Milburn and Gruendel would want to know, so I had prepared myself for a fairly intensive grilling. I had also been wondering what their attitude would be. The circumstances were so strange. They had come all this way to question a journalist whom they obviously would not want to be somewhere in the middle of a deadly serious investigation.

Were they going to feel irritated, put out, or just vaguely discomfited, as Kinane had seemed back in Moscow?

When I came back out on the deck, both agents offered to show me their IDs, but I waved them off. I said that after all this, and with them having come this far, I didn't think they were Russian spies posing as FBI agents. But there I was. Milburn tried immediately to put me at ease. He struck me at the start as quiet, earnest, and straightforward, and I would not change my opinion in the ensuing months. He said first off that he wanted to thank me for passing on the information that Baranov had compiled, and for being willing to continue to act as a middleman until things sorted themselves out. He stressed, without being specific, that the information they had received had been very helpful.

Then he said something that to this day I give him credit for. Among the other things that had made me somewhat apprehensive about this meeting was how they were going to deal with the fact that I was a journalist, and that my intention was to write about this entire episode when the time was right. Instead of avoiding the issue or pretending it didn't exist, Milburn addressed it head-on: "Why," he asked me, "haven't you written this yet?"

I was somewhat taken aback by the directness of the question, but I was glad he asked. I told him the truth. I said we (at the time I meant *Newsweek*) were going to write it. But we would do so when the time was right. I said my feeling was that at this point the story had a good beginning and an interesting middle—after all, here were the three of us together in Crete—but that there was no end yet. I said I needed to see what happened, where this investigation went, before I would write a story.

Milburn, somewhat to my surprise, said that was fair enough. I had worried that I was going to get some kind of quasi-official request not to write about all this, at least not for quite a while. To the contrary, Milburn's question suggested that he understood I was a journalist, and that what journalists do is write stories. (Whether his superiors, or his counterparts in the CIA, shared this opinion was something I was unsure of.)

I said when the time came, when they were in a position to do so, that I would appreciate their cooperation in telling me the parts of the story that I wouldn't know about as it played out. They agreed. But the fact was that none of us knew when that time would come.

The sandwiches and Cokes arrived, and once the waiter had departed, they started the questioning. They avoided going over the material I had already provided. Milburn clearly was familiar with it. He wanted first to know about Baranov's state of mind. How did he seem, emotionally? Was he angry? Frustrated? Was he in control? Was he depressed?

I said that of course he was very angry and frustrated, and for a while I had questioned whether he was in control. There had been occasions in my office when he had spoken despairingly of trying to force his way into the U.S. Embassy, to compel someone to deal with him. I had told him at the time that I thought that probably wasn't a good idea. That he probably wouldn't get in, and that he would seem like a nut, precisely what he wanted to avoid.

I said that his anger was directed mainly at the CIA, that Baranov could not believe how he had been handled while he was an agent back in Moscow. All of this had been detailed in the information he had passed on through me, so I made reference only to the failure to pick up the dead drop. Nor could he fathom why no one had shown the slightest interest in him once he was out of prison, particularly since it was clear to him he had been betrayed.

Gruendel and Milburn listened and took notes. I was looking for their reactions; I was interested in what they were going to be interested in. But it was hard to tell. They weren't reacting much, which I suppose is normal for experienced investigators.

They then moved on to our meetings. When had they started? How often did I see him, and where? I had gone over all this with Kinane, but for whatever reason Milburn wanted to hear it for himself. I told him at first we met mainly in the office, but now had varied that. I told him about the John Bull Pub and the Starlight Diner. He asked what we usually talked about. I said that we had become friends, and having mostly exhausted the details of his case, we often talked about what was in the news. Baranov, I said, was very interested in what was going on in the world and would always pick up a copy of the latest issue of *Newsweek* whenever he visited the bureau.

Milburn then asked about surveillance. Was there any sense we were being watched? That Baranov was being followed? I said that he was the professional, and that he insisted that to date there had been no evidence of surveillance. But I did say that it was certain that the phones in my office were tapped, and that the office itself was probably bugged.

Milburn then requested that in the future we not meet in the office, and that we keep phone contact to a minimum. I said that yes, we'd been trying to do that, and that in the future there would be no meetings at the *Newsweek* bureau.

We had been there for about an hour, Milburn doing most of the questioning, when they turned their attention to Baranov's family. I said he had a wife, two daughters, and a granddaughter, and told them that what I knew of them came only from him. I had never met any of them. I said that from what he had told me, I gathered his wife was very bitter about all that had happened—his agreeing to spy for the CIA, his arrest, and the fact that until now the U.S. government had not seemed interested in him anymore. Still, I said, they were together. I said my impression was that he was still very close to his daughters, and that he plainly adored his granddaughter.

The conversation then took an unexpected turn. They asked whether I thought he would be willing to relocate to the States, whether we had ever spoken of that.

I guess I hadn't expected them to raise this subject because Baranov didn't have a passport. He couldn't get out unless the agency was willing to mount some sort of cloak-and-dagger operation to get him out. The fact that Milburn asked this question indicated that that was clearly being considered in

Washington. It reinforced, once again, the gravity of what I was dealing with, and that again made me uncomfortable, though I tried not to let on in front of the two FBI agents.

I told them that we had in fact discussed this. I said that in the past Baranov had spoken of his desire to move to the United States. He said he thought this would be best for his daughters and granddaughter as well. The problem, I said, was his wife. According to what he had told me on several occasions, she was adamantly opposed to moving. From what I could gather from his descriptions of her, I said she sounded to me like a proud Russian, whose feelings for the way the United States had treated her husband did not incline her to move there. I said however that it seemed to me this was something Baranov would continue working on, because it did seem to be his desire to have them all someday in the United States. But that right now it wasn't going to happen.

They then raised the issue of his passport. Here, for the first time, Milburn revealed a glimpse of his knowledge of the case. He mentioned Baranov's lawyer, Mrs. Kuznetsova, by name. Milburn asked if I had met her. I said unfortunately not. I had tried, in my role as a reporter pursuing this story, to speak to Kuznetsova, as had my colleague in the bureau, Owen Matthews. But she had refused to meet us. Owen, whose Russian was fluent, said his sense was that she had calculated that if the opposing side, that is, the government, found out she was meeting with foreign reporters about this case, it would hardly help her. In this she was no doubt correct.

I said that she had initiated an appellate process to try to get Baranov's passport back earlier than the terms of his parole dictated, which was the summer of 2002. A hearing on the matter had been scheduled, and the government side had not shown up, which meant that the hearing had been rescheduled. Milburn wanted to know when the next hearing was, and what Baranov's sense was of whether he had a chance of winning. I said I wasn't sure about the next hearing date, but that I could let Kinane know when I got back. I also said that Baranov had made it clear he felt he would get nowhere with the appeal, even though he felt that according to the law he should have his passport back. I said he was mainly following through on the legal appeal to prove a point: that even under Boris Yeltsin, his country was not under the rule of law. No matter what the law said, Baranov had told me, a convicted spy in the former Soviet Union would always be treated specially.

About two hours had gone by, and they had no more questions. Milburn said again how grateful he was for my help. He said they would be in touch, via Kinane, and that I should let them know when I was next going to be in the United States. I remember thinking to myself as this meeting ended that there were about one hundred questions I could ask them at this point about the investigation they were obviously in the middle of. But I knew they wouldn't answer them; so I didn't bother. At least not then.

After I walked them back to the lobby, I went to the beach. After a couple of hours I went back to my room, and there was a message from Milburn. They were staying at the hotel next door, and wanted to know whether I wanted to have dinner that night.

I did, if only because I thought maybe I would get to ask a few questions. I called him back, and he said they had rented a car and were going to go down to the nearby village for dinner, and they'd happily swing by my hotel if I wanted to join them.

Fine, I said. So that night the three of us went to a seafood restaurant just by the harbor, and it was clear early on that this was basically a social occasion and not round two of their questioning. It was still awkward, because I knew they were not going to be comfortable answering questions about their investigation.

Even so I quizzed Milburn about the Ames episode, and his involvement in it. I asked about the history of bad relations between the CIA and the FBI, and whether, as some of the books written about the Ames case suggested, that it was—at least to some extent—overcome near the end of the Ames investigation. He said he thought that was true, to some extent. That the people at the agency he worked with were as eager as the FBI people to find out who it was that had sentenced twelve U.S. agents in the Soviet Union to their deaths.

I then brought up, again, Baranov's exasperation (to put it politely) with his CIA handlers. Gruendel volunteered that when she had read the details of his case, she couldn't believe it.

I said far from not being believable, from everything I had read, it seemed depressingly familiar.

And the two FBI mole hunters nodded.

CHAPTER 20

THE BEGINNING OF THE END

I spent a few more days at Elounda Bay after Milburn and Gruendel departed. I was anxious, to say the least, to speak to Baranov, because this meeting had, without question, been a pivotal moment for him. But there was no way I could risk calling him from Crete to say anything about this over the phone.

When I got back to Moscow we arranged to meet at the diner. I recounted in detail the substance of the discussion Milburn, Gruendel, and I had had on the deck overlooking the water. I stressed their interest as to whether he wanted to be relocated. Baranov reiterated to me that he did not want to leave Russia before he got his passport back, since that would mean he would never be able to return, and that was unac-

ceptable to him, and especially to his wife. I said I would re-
peat that message to Kinane the next day at the embassy so that
it was reinforced in Washington.

But for the first time since I had met him, for the first time
since all this had started, I felt that Baranov now believed that
he was going to be vindicated. He smiled frequently as I talked
about the meeting with Milburn and Gruendel, and as we left,
he shook my hand and said how grateful he was for all I had
done. I told him there was more to do, and he nodded. But I
could tell he felt that Washington now believed what he was
telling them.

Milburn had made it clear before he left that for the fore-
seeable future, they didn't think they had any other way to
communicate with Baranov. I was it, and until they could get
me out of the loop—which he stressed they dearly desired—I
needed to stay in touch with Kinane at the embassy. Milburn
had also stressed that they wanted to know when I would next
be in the States, since whenever I visited, they were going to
want to see me.

I had, in truth, become fairly complacent about all this at
this point. Baranov and I had been meeting so frequently, and
over so many months, that any further contact—including any
more meetings with FBI or CIA personnel (which would
come soon enough)—was not going to throw me.

Again, this was probably naïve, and Milburn had made it
clear to me that the bureau did not share my just-another-day-
at-the-office attitude about all this. He had not said that ex-
plicitly, but it was implicit in the instructions. Baranov and I

should vary our meeting locations. We should minimize any phone contact. He had reiterated what Kinane had told me weeks ago, no visits to the office. There were no lectures about how this was very serious business indeed, and that any nonchalance was uncalled for. But it was implicit. The fact that I was in the middle of this had to scare them to death. I was not a spy; I had no idea what the proper tradecraft for any of this was. And indeed both Baranov and I had so violated whatever that tradecraft was that folks in Washington were probably freaking out.

I appreciated the fact that up until this point I had received no lectures from the FBI people—no "You're out of your depth, buddy, so listen up" kind of thing. I think at one level they understood that I wasn't stupid, and that I really wasn't trying to take ridiculous risks. This whole affair had spun out of control quickly (out of control in the sense that if you'd asked me six months earlier whether I would be the only connection between the U.S. government and a key source of information about a high-level mole hunt, I would have thought you were crazy).

At the same time, this whole thing had begun to drive my wife, Kumiko, to distraction. She had said before that she thought I was crazy, and the meeting in Crete, as well as the fact that there didn't seem to be an end to my involvement in sight, only deepened her concerns. She simply thought that I was making assumptions—that the Russians clearly weren't paying attention and that therefore I was at no risk—that I couldn't make. Maybe they were just waiting, she argued. How could they *not* care about someone who was supposedly supplying information about a live mole hunt?

That, indeed, was the key question. But my response at that point was simple: Baranov was the professional. He still had detected no surveillance, and he felt the precautions we were taking on the phone were sufficient. Kumiko was of the view that I was putting my career on the line for a story that was very murky, that in fact might come to nothing much at all.

I didn't necessarily disagree with any of this. But there was also another consideration. The fact was, particularly after the Crete meeting, that I was in too deep to pull out now. Beyond the journalistic considerations was the reality that Baranov was closer than he had been in years to finding some answers, and to getting some sense of justice. I did not believe at this point that there was an alternative for me other than to see this through. Surely the FBI agents weren't deceiving me into thinking I was their only line of communication at the moment. I didn't believe they were kidding when they said their preference was to get me out of the middle. But as far as they could see, there indeed wasn't an alternative. So at the personal level *and* at the journalistic level, I wanted to see this through. Whether it was risky or not, I didn't think I had much choice.

So the spy games continued. Several weeks after Crete, I informed Kinane that I was going to be headed to the United States to give a talk about Russia at an investment conference arranged by a friend of my wife's. It was to be a relatively quick trip, three or four days, but I would be available to meet if Milburn or anyone else desired. Kinane called me back and asked me to come to the embassy for the response. They wanted to know, when I arrived, whether Baranov would consider again relocating to the United States before he received his passport.

This to me suggested two things: one, a level of frustration in not being able to deal with him directly, which meant they were obviously not willing to ask all they needed to know from Baranov with me as the intermediary. That was hardly surprising. No matter how helpful I'd been, this was obviously an extremely sensitive investigation. Indeed, throughout the course of meetings with Milburn and Gruendel, they never ventured anything more than the vaguest generalities as to the state of the investigation, or whether they agreed with Baranov's proposition that the mole, if there was a mole, had to be in the agency. The second thing the request suggested was some urgency. That they needed more information from him now.

I set up a meeting with Baranov. Not to my surprise, he wouldn't budge on the relocation question. At that point it was too important to him and his family to remain Russian citizens, to have the ability to come and go as they pleased. He may have been persona non grata in his own country, but there was no reason his family needed to be. He felt that if he was patient, he would get his passport back under the rules. It seemed important to him that the rules be followed. He wanted the government, this new democratic government, to prove it was a government of laws and not men. He was skeptical as to whether it was, and the passport issue seemed to be his personal litmus test. He believed his passport should have been returned on the basis of the legal arguments he had presented in his appeal in court. But at the least he felt he should get it back when the government *said* he would get it back. The family issue came first, but in my conversations with Baranov, he made it clear that this secondary argument mattered immensely to him. In any case, the answer was no.

I traveled to New York and the next day called Gruendel at the Washington, D.C., Field Office in Buzzard's Bay, out of which she, Milburn, and the entire FBI counterintelligence unit in Washington worked. (Milburn never gave me his phone number, e-mail address, or anything. It was too sensitive for someone in his position to be getting phone calls from a civilian like me, let alone a civilian who was a journalist. All the communication by phone went through Gruendel, and it was only when I was in the United States that I was supposed to call.)

She asked if I had any plans to be in Washington, and I said no. In that case, she said, they'd come up to New York. And the next day they did. I was staying at the Drake Hotel on Park Avenue. We met in the lobby, which was crowded, as was the coffee shop. They asked if there was somewhere else we could talk. I had in fact scoped out a better sight the day before—evidence, I guess, that I was beginning to think a bit like a spy. The IBM Building on Madison Avenue had a spacious lobby in which there was a stand that sold coffee and some tables that were spaced widely apart. It was also echoey, sound traveled up, and while in there the day before, I had had trouble fixing on other people's conversations.

For all their trouble of coming up to New York, this turned out to be a relatively short meeting. I gave them the answer they didn't want to hear. Baranov did not want to relocate without a passport. I asked if there was any progress in coming up with a plan to meet with him directly, and they said the agency was still working on it, but nothing concrete yet, news that was sure to disappoint him. They then asked generally about his well-being, his state of mind, how often we continued to meet. They had no news of substance for him, and the news he had for them, they didn't want to hear. And as for me, I was where I was when all this started, still stuck in the middle.

I went back to Moscow two days later and told Baranov that there was, in effect, no news. He said he wasn't particularly surprised. The next few months would be months of waiting, where patience, for both Baranov and myself, would be a virtue. They would be frustrating months for him. But since I had earned his trust, he began to fill in some of the blanks of his story, provide details that I hadn't yet heard, of what happened after he was recruited, when he returned to Moscow, and when the thing went badly wrong.

CHAPTER 21

PARANOIA

The investigation focusing on the post-Ames mole was intensifying in Washington. The information that Baranov provided, in particular his detailed time line, only reinforced the FBI's belief that someone was out there. Further, like Baranov, the investigators were convinced that the mole was in the agency. More than Vince's ten people knew about Baranov, but not many more, and the FBI was, in the summer of 1999, trying to focus on the most plausible targets. They wanted more information from Baranov; they wanted to question him in great detail. But first they had to figure out a way to do that.

By late 1999, it was time—as the FBI saw it and certainly, despite my journalistic curiosity, as I did—to figure out a way to get me out of the loop. Almost six months had passed from my last contact with anyone in the FBI, and Baranov was again getting extremely restless, worrying that he was again being ignored or, more cynically, that the information he had was so damning that the agency was purposefully not dealing with him.

In this case his cynicism was not justified. Twice, once in February and then in late March 2000, I was asked to come to the embassy to meet with agency agents working out of the Moscow station. This, of course, was highly unusual. Agency people in embassies around the world tend not to be very accessible to journalists, and particularly not when they are trying to deal with a former high-ranking intelligence officer of the U.S.S.R. who had important information to provide about a possible mole at the heart of the U.S. security establishment. To have a journalist in the middle of all this was a nightmare for the agency, for at least two reasons. The first was the possibility that I might actually write something and blow up an ongoing investigation. Second, ever since the Church Committee in the 1970s made public a slew of agency scandals dating back to the fifties, including its use of American journalists stationed abroad, the CIA has rigorously avoided using reporters in anything remotely "operational." If this somehow were to get out, it could easily look as if the agency was up to its old tricks (never mind what it would look like from my standpoint, i.e., the end of my career as a journalist).

Thus, the two meetings in Moscow were short and to the point, though at the time I remember thinking they had a faintly comedic quality. Mike Hurley would usher me into a windowless conference room in a public area near the cafeteria where I had first told him about all this business. A few minutes later, someone would walk in, in the first case a younger guy with short-cropped hair and wire-rimmed glasses who introduced himself only as "Dave." The second time it was a taller, distinguished-looking man who said his name was "Mike." He was, I knew, the deputy station chief, and I already knew what his last name was, even though neither he nor "Dave" would admit to one.

When the meetings ended, they left first and asked me to wait about five minutes. I guess CIA agents were not allowed to be in the embassy cafeteria within yards of a local bureau chief for a U.S. publication. I found myself wondering why it was that two FBI agents in highly sensitive counterintelligence jobs would go out of their way to show me their IDs and not hesitate to tell me their names, while the two agency guys in this case gave me a mild version of the spy-versus-spy schtick.

The answer, I think, is that the schtick is central to the agency; it's so much a part of the agency's mystique that there's no other way for these guys to behave. The culture of secrecy, as the agency's recent history has shown, covers a multitude of sins. It has over the decades enabled it to convey a sense of competence, an image that says, Oh, what we know is so sensitive, and so hot, that you can't know who I am, and god knows, I can't be seen walking within spitting distance of the *Newsweek* reporter here in the embassy cafeteria because that might . . . that might *what,* exactly?

The "I'm a secret CIA guy" act aside, both were friendly. They thanked me for what I had done as an intermediary, and the younger guy, "Dave," even complimented *Newsweek*'s reporting out of Russia in a way that made me think he meant it. At both meetings they wanted to know how Baranov was doing, how his health was holding up, what his state of mind was, whether he had gotten his passport back, whether he had changed his mind about relocating. Both times they conveyed with urgency their desire to get me out of the way. The agency was working on a plan to meet directly with Baranov, but hadn't yet settled on one. But they wanted me out of the way, and soon.

Even if there was no hint of surveillance at my meetings with Baranov, the senior agent said flatly that I was courting danger now.

I didn't think this was melodrama at the time, and I still don't. I told him I didn't need to be convinced. I would be quite happy to be out of the loop. I no longer needed to be persuaded of how serious this all was. His use of the word "danger" jarred me. My wife had been telling me all along that I was putting us in danger and jeopardizing my career in the pursuit of one story.

All along I hadn't believed it. At first, I doubted Baranov's credibility, and then, when I came to believe he was who he said he was, I was deeply skeptical that anything was going to come of this. Third, I got comfortable with Baranov's reassurances, as a "professional," that no one was following us when we met—even though, in the back of my mind, I knew that since I was his only lifeline to the outside world at that point, he could for all I know have been telling me that and then riding home with two KGB goons in the backseat of his taxi.

I had sympathy for his plight, and never had felt comfortable with the idea of extricating myself. I convinced my-self that I had become obliged to him as a person; this was beyond doing someone a favor. He was getting close to being able to set things straight. To bail out on him seemed another betrayal.

But for all that, the last but definitely not least reason I was still in the middle of this was because of the story. This was one that no one else in town had, nor would they. And the more I got sucked into it, the better a story it became. And I knew that if I did just suddenly say to him, "Enough, I'm *way* over the line here, go find yourself another way out of your situation," he might have been so pissed off that he would never talk to me again. And that I couldn't, wouldn't, let happen. I could not let the story get away from me. Baranov, the professional, had recruited me skillfully, knowing what I was after, and I was in for the duration.

When the CIA agent said "danger," a fair bit of this flashed through my mind. This wasn't danger in the sense of covering the war in Chechnya, where journalists were getting killed or kidnapped at an alarming rate. But it was danger nonetheless; there simply was no guarantee that Baranov was right, that we were operating with relative safety. At any point, the KGB could have dropped out of the trees above the Starlight Diner and arrested both of us as we chatted away. Indeed, as the seri-ousness of this affair mounted, the question became more ur-gent: if there *is* a mole, and it's a live mole, why in the world does the Russian government let Baranov continue to meet with an American journalist who could perhaps help establish that mole's existence and possibly even his identity?

So I was ready to be extricated. But even though the CIA deputy station chief pressed upon me the agency's desire to have me sidelined, he didn't ask me to remove myself. Had he, I would have. *That* would have been good enough for me to take to Baranov and say, Slava, sorry old guy, your former employer says it's time for me to go back to writing stories about Boris Yeltsin's liver.

But "Mike" didn't ask me to stand down, because the CIA did not yet have a plan to get directly in touch with their former informant. They still needed me for a while longer, "Mike" asked me if I had plans to be in the United States anytime soon, and I said in fact I was going to be there in the spring, in a couple of months. He said to get in touch with my FBI contacts when I did. Perhaps things would have moved along by then.

CHAPTER 22

SIGN ON THE DOTTED LINE

The CIA's inquiries about Baranov's health that winter and spring of 2000 were not idle. In the months before the meetings, Baranov had been afflicted with a serious, and for a time mysterious, stomach disorder. In March he was admitted to a hospital in central Moscow for a series of tests. The results were not good. At the least he had a severe ulcer—how surprising was that after what he had been through?—and his doctor wanted more tests done to see whether he had stomach cancer.

I visited him frequently in the clinic (it wasn't far from the *Newsweek* office). Unable to keep any food down, he became even more drawn and gaunt. He looked bad, and his mood was not much better. After the biopsy was done, Baranov felt his doctor wasn't being straight with him. In Russia, as in some other countries in which I've worked (Japan most notably), it's not unusual for physicians to flinch from delivering bad news, particularly when it comes to cancer. The doctor would not say whether he had cancer, but he did say that Baranov required major surgery. He was going to need to have about two-thirds of his stomach cut out, and then he would have to live the rest of his life on an extremely bland diet. Baranov took the severity of the treatment as a sign that he must be dying.

I mention this medical history because the timing is critical. It was at a point in which his long wait, our joint effort to get him directly in touch with the U.S. government, was coming close to an end. I think it was partly for this reason that his mood was so black. When I visited him a couple of times a week, he would pad down to the lobby in his green hospital pajamas, looking (particularly after the surgery) like death warmed over, and it was clear to me that he was assuming the worst. I had no independent way to evaluate what he was telling me about his medical condition, but the way he looked made me wonder whether he going to turn out to be a tragic figure, that on the brink of possibly getting the things he wanted—contact with the FBI or CIA, presumably some money for him and his family, and possibly relocation to the United States—he was going to die. Just before his surgery, Baranov had made it clear he was preparing for the worst. Before I left on that day, he shook my hand and asked, with some emotion in his voice, that if he should not survive the surgery, I *not* write his story for *Newsweek*. It would be too much for his family, he said, to have to relive all of this even after he was gone from this earth.

I smiled weakly and said something to the effect that surely this was going to be moot because he'd be fine. But I was shaken, mainly because we had become friends, but also because I was delivering health reports back to the embassy. Kinane had retired to San Francisco, and I was dealing with his deputy. The U.S. government didn't want Baranov to go and die at this point, for reasons that had nothing to do with friendship.

Baranov came through the surgery okay, but his prognosis—according to him anyway—seemed uncertain when I left for the United States that spring. He was desperately hoping that at last I would come back with a plan that would finally get him directly in touch with someone who could take things from here.

When I arrived in New York, I called Lauren Gruendel and told her I was in the States and asked if they wanted to meet. She said yes and she'd call back with the timing. When she did, she said Milburn and she would travel up to New York the next day. I said we could meet again in the IBM building.

They showed up at the appointed hour, Gruendel bought us three coffees, and we sat down. Milburn first wanted to know the status of Baranov's health, and I told them what he had told me about the surgery. His doctor had said it was a "success"; the part of his stomach that needed to be removed had been, and his condition should now improve, under a carefully controlled diet. The guy looked like hell, I told them, but it was possible that the worst was over.

They then told me what we all had been waiting to hear. The agency had come up with a scenario for a direct meeting with Baranov. For all the time it took to get around to this, the

plan revolved around something I had told them months before: that because Baranov could travel without a visa to the
Ukraine, he could then get across the border to the former Soviet republic of Moldova, if that might be a place where the
agency would consider meeting. His Ukrainian friend, Dima,
who lived not far from the border, said it was relatively easy to
drive back and forth without having to stop for a passport
check.

Moldova was acceptable. They now said I was to tell Baranov that he was to try to get to the capital city of Chisinau
anytime after May 15. By then there would be a team of agents
in place waiting for him. He simply needed to go to the U.S.
Embassy, ask for the duty officer, and then give the duty officer a code word. That was it. No cloak-and-dagger stuff; no
elaborate disguises, phony passports, or jumping on and off
umpteen buses. Go to the embassy, ask for the duty officer, give
him a code word, and he would, at long last, be back in the
embrace of the CIA.

Fine, I said, he'll do it; no question. What's the password?

There was, Milburn said, one hitch. In order for me to deliver this message, including passing along the code word, the
agency needed me to sign a document that would state that for
this single operation, I was acting as a CIA asset. The agency
lawyers were insisting on it, Milburn said. If all this was going
to happen, I would have to go "operational."

*　*　*

I don't know why I was so taken aback by this. I don't know why I hadn't seen it coming for months. If anything, the meetings with the two agents in the Moscow embassy should have clued me in as to just how agitated Langley was.

I told them that there would be no problem in my delivering the message; it would be easy, just as every meeting between the two of us had been. I would simply send him an e-mail, using our code for where to meet, and tell him the plan and the password. Done. But the stuff about signing a document and becoming an asset, however briefly, that was likely to be a problem. I told them, look, I'm so far into this that if it were just me, I'd probably go ahead and do it (though I'm not sure I really meant that). But this was something that I was going to have to take up with the editors of *Newsweek* ASAP, and I said I felt it was highly unlikely they would go along with this. If it ever came out that *Newsweek*'s Moscow bureau chief had become, however briefly, an official asset of the CIA, our journalistic peers would crucify us.

Milburn was calm, sensible, and reassuring. He said they understood all that, and were prepared that the answer might come back no. Go talk to your editors, he said, and call us when you have an answer. I said I'd try to do so right away. They said they'd stick in New York for a couple of hours and wait.

I raced back across town to *Newsweek,* whose headquarters is at Fifty-seventh Street between Seventh Avenue and Broadway. This was one of those moments when I *thought* I was thinking the right things about all this, but I really wasn't sure, and I urgently needed the counsel of two trusted colleagues. I barged into Mike Elliott's office; he was the editor of *Newsweek*'s international edition, where 90 percent of my work from Moscow appeared. I said I needed to talk to him and Mark Whitaker, the editor of the U.S. edition, right away.

I must have looked slightly crazed because Mike seemed a little alarmed as he picked up the phone to see if Mark was in his office. I tried to calm down a bit and said, don't worry, Mike, I'm not dying, or quitting, or anything like that; but there is something we need to talk about ASAP, and it has to do with the story about the Russian spy that I've had been working on for so long.

Luckily, Mark was in and available. Mike and I walked into his office and shut the door. Both were aware that I had been working on a project involving a former GRU agent, but of course were not aware of the twists and turns the story had taken. I brought them up to speed and laid out the proposition before us. I told them I felt I was able to pass along the message without risk in Moscow; the issue was the document the agency wanted me to sign. Elliott said it was his view that there was no way I could sign the waiver. If it ever got out, "it would mean the end of your career as a journalist, and it would hurt the magazine." Moreover, he pointed out, it would always give the agency something to hold over me, not a position a foreign correspondent wants to be in. If I was ever going to do a story that made the agency look bad or that they objected to for some reason, they could use this as a way to pressure me.

Whitaker agreed, and I knew they were right. Then Mark

said, why not just tell the FBI to tell the agency people that you won't sign the waiver, but you will deliver the message? See what they say.

I thought this was the right answer, too. If the agency was serious about wanting me out of the way, they'd presumably say thanks but no thanks and come up with a plan B. If however they wanted to get this message to Baranov ASAP and didn't have another way worked out to do it, they might go along.

I called Lauren, and the three of us met about an hour later, again in the IBM atrium. I explained our decision and proposed that we go ahead anyway.

They said they would check with the agency and that Lauren would call me.

Two days later she did. She asked if it was possible for me to go down to Washington for a brief meeting. They would meet me at the shuttle arrival gate. Fine, I said, I'd come down that afternoon.

I had convinced myself that the agency was going to refuse my offer, that the lawyers plainly were in charge now, and they were not going to let this go any further.

Wrong. Milburn said Langley agreed. He repeated the instructions. Baranov is to go to Moldova, show up at the embassy, ask for the duty officer, and utter the words, and the CIA would take it from there. And the magic words were?

"I'm here to see the duty officer—I'm from the media security company."

And that was that. Two days later I boarded a plane back to

Moscow, bearing a message Vyacheslav Baranov had been waiting for since 1992, when he spent his first night in Lefortovo
prison. For him, restitution—and an explanation—awaited. As
for me, I was, save for one last very important meeting, out of
the middleman business.

CHAPTER 23

A TRIP TO MOLDOVA

I met Baranov immediately upon my return at the Starlight Diner. I admit I was a little nervous. I had visions of the nightmare scenario flashing through my head: the KGB swooping down on us at the very moment I was about to give him the password. No, I thought to myself, that kind of stuff only happens in the movies. We sat down and I told him the game plan, where to go and what to say. I told him that the agency had wanted me to go operational and that I had refused. He said that was probably wise, but admitted he was surprised too that the lawyers at Langley had gone along with the plan anyway. He wondered what would have happened if they hadn't. To say he was pleased would be understating by a lot.

He quickly made plans with his Ukrainian friend Dima for a visit, and about a week later set off by train for Kiev. Two days later, they made the trip across the Moldovan border without incident and drove to Chisinau, the capital. They checked into a cheap hotel near the train station, and that afternoon Baranov, ever the professional spy, surveyed the scene around the American Embassy. He saw the entrance he was to go through, and checked for surveillance. He was satisfied that there wasn't any.

The next morning, at ten o'clock, he did as instructed. He was let into the embassy and escorted to a meeting room. There, waiting, was a CIA agent from Langley named Bill, and two men who said they were with the local station. Welcome, Bill said to Baranov, we have a lot to talk about.

When they sat down, Baranov simply asked, "What happened?" Bill said they would get to that, there was plenty of time. First, he said, he wanted on behalf of the agency to apologize. He said that what Vince had told Baranov in Dhaka still stood: that the U.S. government stood behind him, after all these years. He told him that he would be given $10,000 in cash to take with him back to Moscow. And that an offshore bank account was being set up in his name, into which half a million dollars would eventually be deposited.

The CIA was finally starting to make it up to Vyacheslav Baranov, and doing so in a way that to a great extent satisfied him. He hadn't known what to expect of this long-awaited meeting; but the anger and frustration of years ebbed some when he was told of the financial arrangements that were being made on his behalf.

That was the beginning of the business. Bill told Baranov that the next day they would meet at a CIA safe house in the city. He was to be at a certain corner at ten and would be picked up by a man driving a Chrysler Jeep. Then they would go over "what happened," and from the agency's perspective, why it had happened. Then, Baranov could tell them in detail why he was so convinced that there was another mole lurking somewhere in Washington. They were, he was told, eager to hear it, because thanks in part to the information he had provided already via me, the investigation was picking up steam. It was now focused on, but not limited to, the agency.

The meeting came off as planned the following day. Before explaining "what happened," Bill repeated the agency's position that they felt strongly that Baranov and his family should relocate to the United States, particularly given the intensity of the mole hunt underway in Washington. Baranov said he understood, and sympathized, but that it was still not possible. He would leave Russia only with a legal passport in hand, so that he could return legally whenever he wanted to. This, he said, was a matter of principle with him, but it also had a lot to do with his wife, who refused to take part in any discussion about leaving her native country. To his relief, he was assured that none of this affected the agency's financial commitment to him.

As for what happened. Baranov was told of a CIA that in the early 1990s was reeling from the damage inflicted by, as it turned out, Aldrich Ames. An atmosphere of paranoia had gripped Langley and the Moscow station as so many Soviet spies got rolled up. Baranov replied that he had come to understand the damage Ames had done, but that it still didn't explain the "unprofessionalism" of how he was handled in Moscow.

The man from the CIA told Baranov that there had been questions back at Langley about his bona fides. Some felt the KAL 007 information was enough to establish his credibility, but others did not. Mike, upon his return from Moscow, had backed him, but there were doubters. This infuriated Baranov. How could he have been given precise instructions to follow in Moscow if the agency was still debating whether he was real or not? How could he leave a dead drop and then find it still sitting there days later? What was the point of all that if they thought he was a "dangle"?

They had no answer. They were not justifying anything.

Baranov will go to his grave with not a lot of respect for the CIA. He insists neither the KGB nor the GRU would ever in a million years have acted like this. But it was clear to me, upon his return, that much had changed. The seething bitterness that lay behind so many of our conversations had abated. He smiled more. I had described him once to one of my editors as a clenched fist of a man. He no longer seemed like that when he came back from Chisinau. He had already bought some new clothes and a fancy pair of designer sunglasses.

He had come in from the cold, and the basic fact was, he had me to thank for that. He now had most of what he had sought. He had the apology he felt he was owed, and it had seemed heartfelt. He had money in the bank, with more coming. He knew his family could relocate at the CIA's expense to the United States whenever they wanted, if they wanted. And he knew, finally, that the powers that be in Washington were well aware that he was right: that he had been betrayed. The information he had provided had kick-started what had been a slow-moving investigation, but was now more intense and getting more so. Baranov, of course, wanted to know who had done him in almost as much as the FBI and the CIA did. The question left on the table was, would he—and they—ever find him?

CHAPTER 24

"SPIES CATCH SPIES"

An FBI agent named Ray Mislock, for years the bureau's Soviet section chief, charged with identifying and deterring Moscow's agents operating in the United States, had a saying that he repeated to his troops over and over: "Spies catch spies." It is a truism in the intelligence world. The best way to know if Moscow has a spy in Washington is to hear it from someone at the KGB, or the GRU, who knows it for certain. But that simple logic is also what often sends the spying game straight down the *Alice in Wonderland* rabbit hole. The people who run spies worry endlessly about whether the information from the people they have recruited is genuine, or whether it is the work of someone posing as an informant, someone who is actually in the business of supplying disinformation.

In the murky world of counterintelligence, the suspicions and fears are even more intense among those who try to determine if there are spies in their midst. They are the mole hunters, and for them figuring out whom they can trust—and whom they can't—is the essence of the game. It is a slippery, frustrating business. An old joke has a counterintelligence officer looking at himself in the mirror and wondering, who does that guy work for?

An investigation—a mole hunt such as the one Baranov and I were in the middle of—is driven by that single question. Neither of us knew the full scope of the investigation we were connected to when he returned to Moscow from Chisinau. It had become vast, it turned out, involving over sixty FBI agents, and just as in the pursuit of Ames, it included several people from the CIA helping in the pursuit of someone they feared was one of their own. The information Baranov had already passed on— much of which he repeated during his meetings in Chisinau— had helped convince all involved that they were not chasing a ghost, that there *was* a post-Ames mole lurking somewhere. As Milburn later put it, the details he provided about his case "convinced everyone that there was no other answer."

In Chisinau, Baranov added to his story certain things that he had not yet shared with me (and thus had not yet been turned over to the FBI). Even before he had learned from me that Aldrich Ames was gone from his position in Washington in 1989 and thus no longer in a position to know about his recruitment that same year, Baranov was convinced he had been sold out. Vince had assured him that only ten people would know his identity. For that reason Baranov was strongly inclined to think it had to have been an agency mole who had betrayed him. But that wasn't the only reason. In the Chisinau safe house, he told the agency people present about the KGB's "cooperation" with the Russian newsmagazine show *Top Secret,* which he had agreed to be interviewed for while he was a prisoner at Perm 35.

Spies, good ones anyway, are detail-oriented. Scraps of information help solve puzzles, so they are trained to pay attention. When Baranov sat in Perm in the autumn of 1995, his jailers allowed him to watch the broadcast of the sensational account of his arrest by the KGB on network television. It was a deeply humiliating experience for him. But it was also, he told the two agents in Chisinau, unintentionally illuminating. One thing had leapt out at him: when the dramatic, black-and-white footage of him going into that phone booth in Moscow to leave his message for Mike was shown, he recognized the tape had been edited for the broadcast. Specifically, the date and time of the filming that had appeared in the lower left-hand corner when he was shown the original tape during his interrogation—"15 06 90, 12.47" (15 June 1990, 12:47 P.M.)—had been deleted. And the voice-over on the broadcast said that the arrest had come after careful shadowing by the KGB, and that Baranov had entered the phone booth in July of 1992.

This was not so, of course, but it was telling. Why, Baranov asked his interviewers in Chisinau, would the KGB want to create the impression that the events of June 1990 took place two years later? The answer, he said, was that they wanted it to appear as if its crack investigators had doggedly tracked him down after almost three years of legwork. Why? All this "elaborate staging," Baranov continued, was for the single purpose of protecting someone. The average Russian viewer could not have cared less when the video of Baranov was shot. But if the CIA's operatives in the Moscow embassy were watching—and they were—to reveal the actual date the video was taken (the summer of 1990) would have told Washington that the KGB had been on to Baranov almost as soon as he returned from Dhaka. And the immediate question would have been, how was that possible? Ames was already in jail, so by then the American mole hunters knew that he hadn't given Baranov away. But they didn't yet know who had, or whether, in fact, *anyone* had. Other theories were then in play, including the possibility that there had been some kind of technical penetration—an intercepted message, perhaps. Moscow was scarcely going to give the Americans hard evidence that there was another mole. By creating the appearance that it had taken more than two years of detective work to get to his arrest, the KGB was covering up the fact that someone had given him up.

Baranov did not know it, but now he was preaching to the choir. In Washington, in the second half of 1999, the mole hunt had intensified, thanks in part to Baranov's reemergence and the information he had provided. It homed in on a single suspect in the CIA, a man who was in a position to know about Baranov's recruitment and a handful of other "blown" agency operations. An FBI official named Tim Caruso, who was overseeing the investigation, believed that this official, who had for sixteen years worked in the Directorate of Operations, the most secret part of the agency, was the man they were looking for.

CIA officials agreed. They had information received from a source in Moscow, a man who was on their payroll. He told the CIA that there was an informant for Moscow working in Washington who operated under the code name "B." Among other things, the Moscow source said the American spy frequently left information in dead drops in a Northern Virginia park called Nottaway. The agency suspect lived near the park and jogged there frequently. This was circumstantial evidence (the bureau would need direct evidence of this man's espionage in order to arrest him), but it was nonetheless compelling.

For a time, this official believed he was going to be indicted. But as the investigation progressed, to the FBI's embarrassment, the case fell apart. The investigators had found a map of Nottaway Park with a bunch of numbers the agent had scribbled on it. It turned out to be his jogging map; the numbers, the amount of time it took him to run from one point to another. ("What are you doing with my jogging map?" he inquired when shown what the bureau men thought was a piece of incriminating evidence.) He passed a lie detector test; there was no evidence of any extra income coming in or any unusual spending patterns. He was not the man they were looking for. The mystery of who had given Baranov up remained.

Milburn and the others involved in the investigation had focused on the CIA in part because it was where most of those who knew of Baranov's recruitment worked. The number of people outside the agency who would know the identity of such a valuable agent might be counted on one hand.

Still, they did look elsewhere. In February 1999, in fact, one of Milburn's colleagues in counterintelligence, an agent named Robert Kimmel, argued to Director Louis Freeh that they could not rule out the possibility that there was a spy in the bureau's own ranks. Freeh asked Kimmel to write a memo spelling out why he thought so.

Kimmel based some of his argument on how the Soviets had handled a bureau agent named Earl Pitts, a counterintelligence officer who had been arrested as a Soviet spy in 1996. In the debriefing following his arrest, Pitts had said he thought there was another penetration of the bureau. When he worked in the bureau's counterintelligence office in New York in the late 1980s, the Soviets had never asked him for certain specific information that they knew he was privy to, and that had puzzled him. This led him to suspect that perhaps there was someone else providing the information. In a meeting at bureau headquarters with Freeh, Kimmel also cited classified information that he has said buttressed his argument. Freeh then asked his national security division for an assessment. For reasons that remain unclear, they ultimately rejected the idea that there was another mole in the bureau after Pitts had been arrested in 1996.

So Milburn and the others persisted. Well into the middle of 2000 they believed Baranov's loss could only be attributed to an agency mole.

* * *

Baranov's regular meetings with the agency ended in the late summer of 2000. He had told their representatives all he had. Now he waited for news. Sometime in the second half of 2000 the CIA and the FBI got what felt like a gift from the gods. Or rather, from someone a lot like Vyacheslav Baranov. He was a former high-ranking official in the SVR (a successor agency of the KGB), an active, still valuable mole who, as this is written, remains on the CIA's payroll, apparently unknown to the Russian government.

It was this agent who had provided the information about Agent B and the Nottaway Park dead drops. When that case fell apart, the agency pressed the source for more information, and he proved highly industrious in response. Plowing through the SVR's storage room in its Moscow headquarters, he found a remarkable set of documents. It was the entire case history of an American agent who had apparently started working for the Soviet Union in 1985. He had risen through the ranks of his agency, and had attained a highly sensitive position in the U.S. intelligence community. Though the documents referred to the agent by a variety of code names, there were fingerprints on some of the files that had been handled by the spy. To the astonishment of Jim Milburn and the others, he was in the FBI. He was one of them. His name was Robert Hanssen.

This revelation was devastating to the FBI. Hanssen had seemed like the perfect FBI agent. He was a staunch Catholic, a member of the intensely devout Opus Dei sect of Catholicism, and a dedicated family man, the father of six children. Unlike Aldrich Ames, he had lived modestly, which helped to cover his tracks for more than fifteen years. But in February of 2001, the FBI arrested him.

Baranov was in Moscow at the time, and I was in Beijing, where I had taken up my next assignment. We were both electrified by the news, assuming that this was probably his man. But we were puzzled, too. It was not clear how Robert Hanssen could have known about Vyacheslav Baranov. An FBI counterintelligence officer should *not* know about CIA recruits in foreign countries.

The more I thought about this, the more I began to think that maybe Hanssen wasn't Baranov's man. I was desperate to know, though. And so obviously was Baranov. I called Lauren Gruendel in Washington and, in as roundabout a fashion as I could, asked whether the "recent news" was what a certain friend of ours had been waiting for. I expected her to say no. She paused and said, "No, it's not."

I said something like, "It's not?" The implication was clear. If it wasn't Hanssen, then it had to be someone else— that is, yet *another* mole beyond Ames, and now beyond Hanssen.

Gruendel hesitated. This was not a call I should have made, and she shouldn't have been talking about this stuff on the phone. But she also knew my curiosity was understandable, and finally she said, "Look, we don't know yet."

*　*　*

Robert Hanssen was an extraordinarily skillful mole. It turned out he started spying for Baranov's employer, the GRU, in 1979. Then, after a two-year hiatus, he began reporting to the KGB. He was in a very valuable position for them. From 1981 to 1985, he worked as an analyst in the FBI's Soviet analytical division; then he went to New York for two years to hunt Soviet spies at the United Nations; then he returned to Washington in 1987 where, again in the Soviet division, he had broad access to intelligence secrets across agencies of the U.S. government.

Among other things, he told the Soviets about a tunnel that the FBI had built under the Soviet Embassy in Washington in order to plant listening devices. He confirmed information that Ames had provided Moscow with about three U.S.-based Soviet agents who had been recruited as double agents by the FBI. Two of them were executed, and one did fifteen years in the Gulag. It was Hanssen who enabled the Soviets to tip off an alleged spy they had in the State Department, a diplomat named Felix Bloch against whom the bureau had painstakingly built a case. He was warned that he was under suspicion, and the bureau was never able to arrest him. To this day the mole hunters are bitter about it.

At the time of Hanssen's arrest in early 2001, I read all the stories in the American press about him with a sense of disorientation. They made much of the fact that the CIA and the FBI had been convinced that there was another mole. Story after story said that there had been unexplained intelligence losses that could not be attributed to Ames. The most prominent case mentioned was Bloch's. The stories focused heavy attention on the loss of the tunnel.

None of them, of course, mentioned Baranov. But I knew that he was very much on the minds of Jim Milburn and the other members of the investigating team. In the intelligence world, Felix Bloch was a former State Department functionary. Even if the allegations against him were true, the secrets he had passed on to Moscow could not, in an intelligence officer's mind, compare to the *potential* gold Baranov would have been in a position to deliver to Washington. A full colonel in the GRU, in Moscow, with a career trajectory that suggested higher positions awaited, *that* was a very big fish indeed. The press accounts went on and on about Felix Bloch, but in the minds of both the mole hunters and the CIA, Felix Bloch was chump change compared to the loss of a GRU colonel.

I told Baranov what Gruendel had said. We had found a way to communicate by sending encrypted e-mail messages that he felt were secure. He found it very difficult to believe that someone so removed from the CIA's operations abroad could have been the one to finger him. He had heard nothing from the CIA since the meetings in the late summer of 2000.

Like Ames before him, Hanssen cut a deal to save his life: he would tell in intimate detail what he did during more than twenty years of spying, in exchange for getting life in prison, rather than the death penalty. In the summer of 2001, he was sentenced, and his debriefing began. It continues as this is being written, but for Baranov there apparently was an answer.

Robert Hanssen, like the SVR agent in Moscow who ultimately sent the FBI to his doorstep, was an industrious spy, and he was a geek. Unlike many of his counterparts in the Soviet analytical division (particularly those who were, like him, over fifty years old), he mastered the twenty-first-century black art of computer hacking. Armed with that skill, he had ranged far and wide through American intelligence secrets. The information that he would know about in the course of his regular duties would have been interesting enough to his paymasters. He was aware, for example, of which Russian agents stationed in the United States were in fact on Washington's payroll. He knew which Soviet spies stationed in the United States Washington was targeting for possible recruitment. He told the Soviets about FBI-run disinformation operations in the United States (including one in particular in which Moscow thought it was getting valued intelligence from a U.S. military officer). He was also aware of what CIA assets, men such as Baranov, had told both agency and FBI debriefers once they had been brought in from the cold—brought back to the United States once their careers, for whatever reasons, were at an end.

This was a lot, but for Hanssen it was only a start. His ability to hack into places that he should not have had access to enabled him, in 1987, to pass on a top-secret report assessing the relative nuclear-war-fighting capability of the United

States and the Soviet Union. He had apparently lifted that report from the computers of the National Security Council. He also revealed an extraordinary array of material from what is supposed to be the most secret—and computer savvy—agency in the U.S. government: the National Security Agency. (One example: Hanssen acquired a report detailing some of the methods the NSA uses to listen in on foreign governments.)

But to mole hunters like Jim Milburn, the question of Baranov remained. Could Hanssen possibly have given him up, even though it appeared he was not in a position to have direct knowledge of his recruitment? Hours of Hanssen's extraordinary, lengthy debriefing were spent on the subject, and the results were at best inconclusive. Hanssen said the code name "Agent Tony," recruited somewhere on the subcontinent, was familiar, but he insisted he couldn't be sure.

Several of his interrogators didn't believe this response. Did he or did he not give up this agent? Hanssen said he couldn't be sure, and wouldn't be shaken from his story. He said he had over the years given away so much information that there were some things he could not remember.

Milburn, for his part, came to believe that Hanssen had not betrayed Baranov, that he simply could not have gotten access to the name, not matter how deft he might have been at cracking computer files that were supposed to be off limits to him. Others do not agree.

The question of trust in the spying game never goes away—not even after a spy has pleaded guilty and agreed to "cooperate." There are some on the Hanssen debriefing team who suspect Hanssen is feeding them disinformation, acknowledging the *possibility* that he may have given up Baranov, perhaps in order to shield yet *another* informant within the U.S. intelligence community. Hanssen, after all, once boasted to his handlers in Moscow that he was "insanely loyal" to them, and some of his former colleagues believe that loyalty continues.

Much about the Hanssen story remains murky. Was it really true that Moscow had no idea where he worked—let alone who he was—all those years? That no Russian agent ever clandestinely photographed him making a dead drop? That is what the FBI appears to believe. An internal, highly critical bureau postmortem on the case revealed that in 1993 the Russians actually complained when someone identifying himself as a "disaffected FBI agent" tried to peddle U.S. secrets to a Russian intelligence officer. (Hanssen had temporarily broken off his work for Moscow in 1991.) The Russians complained to the State Department because their Washington embassy felt this was a trap—a way to snare one of its operatives and have him thrown out of the country. This kind of gamesmanship was standard during the Cold War, and the resulting complaint was simply part of the game. But the FBI report says Hanssen in 1993 used the same name—Ramon Garcia—that he had used when he started spying for Moscow in 1985. Yet the bureau believes Russia never put two and two together and figured out that their precious mole was in the FBI.

More serious is the mystery of how Hanssen was apparently able to crack into highly sensitive computer systems well beyond those he was supposed to have access to. Could he really have come across Baranov's name simply by trolling through shockingly vulnerable computers somewhere in the U.S. national security *apparat*? Could the CIA's systems be *that* vulnerable?

Baranov remained skeptical of the Hanssen story, and he was relieved to hear that an investigation continues. There are, in fact, intelligence losses, Baranov aside, that cannot be ascribed to Hanssen. The immediate elation and excitement he felt when Hanssen was arrested is gone. Vyacheslav Baranov, it is true, has now got most of what he wanted: an apology from the U.S. government, financial security, and a promise that he can relocate to the United States if he chooses to. But still he doesn't think he's heard a convincing answer to the question that obsesses him: If not Hanssen, who?

As late as spring 2002, Milburn and others were pursuing the question, which they still consider open. If Hanssen's hacking didn't unearth Baranov's name in some vulnerable computer file, then someone else is guilty of burning Baranov. There is—or was—a mole. A very well-placed mole, probably burrowed exactly where Baranov has insisted it was all along: somewhere in the CIA. And even if Hanssen was able to point the KGB toward Baranov, Milburn and others in the FBI acknowledge that there are reasons to believe that someone else did too. (After all, both Ames *and* Hanssen fingered former GRU general Dmitry Polyakov.) But the maddening truth, both for Baranov and the mole hunters he has helped, is that they—and we—may never know the truth. Spies catch spies— sometimes. But not always.

EPILOGUE

Vyacheslav Baranov spent much of 2002 in Moscow, often with his wife, Tatyana, at a new dacha he had built with the funds given him by the CIA after he came in from the cold. There was, in fact, a marked change in Baranov's lifestyle once he got some money from the CIA—guilt money, I call it. Going from near poverty to having $500,000 in a Swiss bank account would create change in anyone's life. But Baranov began to wear clothes that were slightly flashy—a designer jacket, Italian sunglasses—and then he built the dacha. Everything else considered, it was hard to begrudge him any of this; but one must also consider its timing and context. Vladimir Putin, an ex-KGB man himself (a former intelligence officer overseas and not a "knuckle dragger") had succeeded Boris Yeltsin on millennium eve—December 31, 1999. Baranov had received this news with trepidation, believing, as I did, that it represented a lurch back toward a police state. Though Putin has cracked down on some liberties, most notably press freedoms, the worst fears about him have so far been exaggerated. But at that point, in the late spring and early summer of 2000, it was too early to draw any conclusions. And I believed Baranov was drawing unwise attention to himself.

Consider his circumstances then. He was a convicted spy,

and a former KGB man had taken over as president of Russia. Since getting out of prison, Baranov provided the U.S. government with helpful information in pursuit of a suspected mole. I told him before I left Moscow that I didn't think his rather obvious display of new wealth was wise. What if the tax authorities come and ask you where you got the money to build the dacha?

His answer basically was that this was something he was doing for his Tanya. His wife had suffered so over the years, and she had always dreamed about having a classic dacha in the quiet woods outside Moscow. This was particularly important to her since they had a grandchild.

All understandable. And he wasn't going to listen to my advice anyway. There still have been no signs that anyone in Moscow is paying attention—just as no one, apparently, paid attention to us during the nearly three years we were meeting there.

If there is a question that we have asked ourselves, and which I have discussed with a few friends and colleagues over the years, it is this: Given how frequent our meetings were and given that Baranov possessed information of significant value to the U.S. government as it hunted down a Russian spy, why did the Russians let us get away with it? Why was there never any indication, at least as far as Baranov could tell, of surveillance? Why didn't the government kick me out for impersonating a spy? Why was the CIA's paranoia about meeting Baranov in Russia, as well as its concern about my meetings with him, apparently misplaced? Why didn't *something* happen?

For what it's worth, here is what I think the answer is: I believe Baranov's story reflects the collapse of the Russian state. It's not just that Russia isn't a police state. Under Yeltsin, and in particular during his second term, which is when I worked in Moscow, Russia barely functioned as a state at all. It couldn't collect the taxes to pay its teachers or doctors or firemen or military officers. Everywhere the symbols of a superpower were collapsing: think of the *Mir* space station, whose constant near calamities became the butt of Jay Leno's jokes on *The Tonight Show*. Think of the *Kursk* submarine whose poor crew perished when one of the sub's torpedoes accidentally exploded.

Corruption, meanwhile, was everywhere. Everything was for sale, including influence to the Yeltsin inner circle; and in this environment a handful of businessmen, who came to be known as the "oligarchs," made vast amounts of money by fleecing the Russian state.

In that environment, any smart intelligence officer (or counterintelligence officer) could see what was going on. You could sit around and hope to get paid, or you could try to get a piece of the new action for yourself.

That's what many or most of the smart ones did. Anyone with half a brain in the former KGB and GRU let themselves get "privatized." The spies went to work for the businesses that the oligarchs put together after the Soviet Union collapsed. The new business establishment organized huge intelligence operations that they used to spy on the government and on each other. Those left in the intelligence agencies were bureaucrats working with outdated technology and no clear mandate.

So it's our belief, his and mine, that Baranov slipped through the cracks. Once he got out of Perm 35, he was off the KGB's radar. It would be nice to think that a reformed country, a former police state turned democracy, was simply leaving alone a guy who had committed a crime but done his time. I don't think that was the case. If the government had known what he was up to, it obviously would have cared. I just don't think it noticed as we met in the Starlight Diner and I passed on the code words that enabled him to meet with his former CIA masters and help in the pursuit of a Russian agent.

The few colleagues and friends who know about this story also often ask another question: Do you really think this was the right thing to do? Even though it turned out okay in the end, don't you think it could have gone very badly for all concerned? I was aware of the risks all along, though maybe not aware enough. There is a moment that gives me pause. It's the meeting with FBI agents Milburn and Gruendel in Crete. Since the arrest of Robert Hanssen, there is something I have thought about a lot: What if it hadn't been Milburn there that day but Hanssen? What if one of the people in whom I was confiding as Baranov's intermediary had been a double agent? Hanssen had been in counterintelligence at the bureau, just as Milburn is. The fact that the most significant post-Ames mole to date turned out to be in the FBI makes the risks I was taking seem more real as I reflect on them than they did at the time. I trusted Milburn, and I probably would have trusted

Robert Hanssen. I wanted to see how this story was going to end, and I wanted the U.S. government to make amends to Baranov, who I thought had been screwed.

This question—What if I had been dealing with Hanssen?—is not idle. Because it turns out Robert Hanssen had heard of Vyacheslav Baranov, if not by name then at least by the details of his case. U.S. investigators told me in May 2002, after the debriefing of Hanssen was complete, that Moscow Center had been made aware of Baranov's trip to Moldova—the one that I helped arrange—and was fed a full report about the former GRU colonel's debriefing there. It was Robert Hanssen who did the feeding. He did not name Baranov by name during his debriefing, and it remains maddeningly unclear if Hanssen could have known about Baranov in the early nineties, when he was arrested. But he did apparently know about the Moldova trip, and perhaps even how it came about.

This was a chilling thing to find out, of course. Here I was, playing these cloak-and-dagger games with a former spy who had betrayed his country, in order to find out who in turn had betrayed *him*—and it turned out that our whole "operation" had been betrayed.

That fact, of course, raises even more questions. If Moscow did find out what Baranov was up to, why hasn't it done anything about it? However lax and corrupt the newfangled KGB may be, surely the information about Baranov's trip to Moldova had to be of concern to it, particularly if there were a live mole still in play somewhere in Washington. Here the questions just pile up, and I am afraid I do not have the answers. One obvious conclusion would be that the whole matter is a dead letter. Whoever it was who betrayed Slava Baranov—and everyone involved agrees he was betrayed—that person must either be dead, sitting in a dacha outside Moscow, or on a tropical island somewhere with a fat bank account. But that conclusion raises another question: If the Russians don't care, why do the FBI and the CIA? Why is there an ongoing investigation, if the matter is dead? Precisely *because* the Baranov investigation remains active as this is written, people like Milburn are constrained from answering that question. The truth is, I don't know what the answer is. But as I write this I don't believe the Baranov mystery will ever be solved.

There is a last question. And that is about Baranov's motivation. Why did he agree to spy for the CIA? And why was he so determined not to be left in the cold? One of the things that intrigued me about him was that all along I felt that part of the reason he felt so betrayed by what happened to him is that he really seemed to have a heartfelt admiration for what we, as Americans, like to think of as the best parts of our country: the rule of law and freedom of expression and a broad array of other civil liberties. He had never been to the United States, but he admired it. All that seemed genuine. But it's also true, of course, that there was the prospect of monetary gain and, eventually, a comfortable life in the United States.

I think it was some combination of both. Yes there was some greed involved, but I also believe he was disgusted with "the system," as he called the Soviet Union. How can I be sure he wasn't just telling me what he thought I wanted to hear?

For all his cynicism about his country, he waited more than two years to see if a Russian court would finally give him his passport back so he could leave for the United States legally. He could have been in this country in the summer of 2000 had he abided by the CIA's urgings that he leave Russia as soon as possible.

All true. But it is also true that his daughters, and the Baranovs' beloved granddaughter, now live here. They agreed, in the summer of 2001, to relocate, believing with their father (and to the distress of their mother) that their future would be better here. Then came September 11. For a few weeks they debated, within the family and with the CIA, whether it was still a good idea to come. Then they stuck by their decision. And in late September they boarded a plane in Moscow and moved to the United States, courtesy of American taxpayers. I was in New York at the time, helping *Fortune* write about the monstrous events of the 11th, and like everyone else trying to cope with it. I felt heartened that they had come; it was a hopeful sign, an affirmation of a basic fact. For all the supposed hatred and envy of the United States that we have been reading about in the wake of September 11, there is a reason why the longest visa lines in the world are those outside of American consulates.

Baranov eventually followed. In the summer of 2002, Tanya finally agreed to relocate to the United States so the family could stay together. Then, in late August, the Russian government, at the urging of the GRU and the FSB, again refused to give Baranov his passport. He then reluctantly agreed to a

CIA-devised "extraction" plan, one that was familiar to him and to me. In early September, he drove Tanya and Alisa, the granddaughter who had spent the summer at their dacha, to Sheremetyevo airport and put them on a commercial flight to New York. Then Baranov made his escape, using the same route by which he managed to reunite with the CIA two years earlier: a train to the Ukraine, then a ride across the border to Moldova. By mid-September, he was in the Washington area, staying with his daughters, beginning a new life in the United States. It was where he wanted to be, even if it had taken longer than he ever dreamed it would to get here.

The life of a spy, a real spy, can be as bitter and lonely as those that John Le Carré portrays in his novels. Baranov is a man now loathed in his own country as a traitor, and had been abandoned by the country to which he pledged his services. That's the very unglamorous reality of spying. The idealized picture he had in his head about the United States and the way it does business didn't include getting tossed aside by the CIA as if he didn't exist. The agency showed, in its way, what it thought of its Joe. Was that any different from what it—or any other intelligence service—thinks about any asset that gets burned? You win some, you lose some. And a double agent is a double agent. Go down that road and some money may flow your way, but don't expect a lot of respect.

Vyacheslav Baranov's life as a spy is over now—his value to the U.S. mole hunt used up—and he has a more comfortable life to show for it. But at an extraordinary price. If he had to do it all over again, I feel sure he wouldn't.

INDEX

INDEX

INDEX

India, 33, 35–36
Inside Soviet Military Intelligence (Suvorov), 23,
    104–6
intelligence, Soviet, *see* GRU; KGB
intelligence, U.S., *see* CIA; FBI
Italy, 125

journalists, 9–10, 162
    cooperation with CIA, 125–42, 143–59,
        161–66, 168–79, 182, 196–99
    embassies and, 162
    see also press; *specific publications*
Journey into the Whirlwind (Ginzburg), 113

KAL 007 incident, 52–53, 63–66, 90–91, 100,
    104, 178
Karla myth, 24
KGB, 3–4, 5, 13, 23, 24, 27, 29, 38, 45, 47, 62,
    70, 84, 85, 96, 175, 178, 183, 195, 196
    arrest, interrogation, and trial of Bara-
        nov, 4–6, 19, 20, 87–107, 183
    counterintelligence, 72–74, 77, 82,
        87–94, 101–3, 164, 184
    coup attempt against Gorbachev, 66–67,
        84, 85
    post-Soviet, 96–99, 101–7, 111–12, 119,
        197–200
    "sweep teams," 71
    U.S. spies working for, 189–94
Khasbulatov, Ruslan Imranovich, 107
Khrushchev, Nikita, 21
Kiev, 119–20, 175
Killer Spy (Maas), 124n., 144–45
Kimmel, Robert, 186
Kinane, Bill, 130–32, 135–42, 144, 146, 148,
    151, 154, 155, 156–57, 169
Korea, 52–53, 63
Krasyanov, Anatoly, 113
Kudrin, Mikhail, 101–2
Kursk submarine, 197
Kuznetsova, Tatyana Georgevna, 98–100,
    104–7, 113, 150–51

labor camps, 4–5, 6, 7, 12, 13, 20, 30, 91,
    107–9, 111–15, 119, 183, 189
Latvia, 21, 22
Le Carré, John, 24, 202
Lefortovo Prison, Moscow, 95–96, 107, 109,
    114
Lenin, Nikolai, 22–23

London, 42, 58

Maas, Peter, *Killer Spy*, 124n., 144, 145
Matthews, Owen, 3–4, 150
Middle East, 126
Mike, 70, 71–75, 78, 82, 92, 102–3, 124, 178
"Mike," 163, 166
Milburn, Jim, 109, 117, 140–42, 144–52, 153,
    154, 157, 169–74, 182, 185–87, 190,
    192, 194, 198, 199, 200
Military Collegium, 101
Military Diplomatic Academy, Moscow, 22, 25
Ministry of Security, 87
Mir space station, 197
Mislock, Ray, 181
Moldova, Baranov's trip to, 170, 173, 175–78,
    182–83, 199–200
mole hunters, 109, 117–18, 122, 125, 136–42,
    144–58, 161–66, 169–74, 182–94,
    198–200, 202
Molykov, Gennadi Andreavich, 87–88, 89–93
money laundering, 145
Moscow, 1, 5, 10, 15, 25, 27–29, 33, 36, 42,
    46, 47, 55, 62, 65, 158
    CIA station in, 69–83, 91, 92, 99, 148,
        165–66, 171, 177–78
    Lefortovo Prison, 95–96, 107, 109, 114
    post-Soviet, 1–3, 96–99, 128–42, 197
    Sheremetyevo Airport arrest of Baranov,
        84, 85–87, 93
    U.S. embassy, 12, 82, 121, 123, 128–36,
        147, 162

Nagorski, Andy, 4–5, 6, 113–14
National Security Agency, 192
National Security Council, 192
NATO, 30, 37, 39, 58
    weaponry and technology, 30–32, 37,
        191–92
Nazism, 17–18, 19
Newsweek, 1, 3, 6, 8, 11, 15, 104, 114, 124,
    126, 128–29, 133, 146, 148–49, 163,
    168, 171–72
New York, 158–59, 169–72, 186, 189
    September 11 terrorist attacks, 13, 201
Nightmover (Wise), 124 and *n.*, 141
Nottaway Park, 185, 187
nuclear weapons, 21, 128, 191–92

Ottawa, 120–21

- 206 -

INDEX